SCOTLAND

ALASTAIR SCOTT

Top 10 Scotland Highlights

The Top 10 of Everything

CONTENTS

Scotland Area by Area

Streetsmart

Within each Top 10 list in this book, no hierarchy of quality or popularity is implied. All 10 are, in the editor's opinion, of roughly equal merit.

Front cover and spine Stunning setting of the 13th-century Eilean Donan Castle in the Highlands
Back cover Aerial view over the historic centre of Edinburgh from Calton Hill
Title page Colourful harbour-front houses in Tobermory, Isle of Mull

Welcome to
Scotland

Shimmering lochs, silent glens, romantic castles, remote islands, riotous festivals, drams of whisky and rounds of golf. The birthplace of "Rabbie" Burns and Harry Potter is a proud nation, and no wonder: Scotland has fuelled the passions of artists, writers and adventurers for centuries. With Eyewitness Top 10 Scotland, it's your turn to be inspired.

It may be small, but few countries can match Scotland's mix of scenic splendour and cultural heritage. What could be more romantic than crossing the sea to the **Isle of Skye**, more moving than seeing the site of the **Glencoe** massacre or more exciting than joining the crowds thronging the streets during the world-famous **Edinburgh International Festival**? And what could be more thrilling than watching ospreys in the **Cairngorms National Park**, monster-spotting for "Nessie" on **Loch Ness**, or exploring fairy-tale **Glamis Castle** – supposedly one of the most haunted places in Britain?

Scotland has long attracted thrill-seekers, who come to "bag" a Munro or to hike the **West Highland Way**. Yet we love its gentler activities too, such as dolphin-spotting on the Moray Firth or strolling amongst the exotic plants of **Inverewe Gardens**. Its cultural attractions are equally varied: Impressionist paintings as well as Dolly the Sheep in Glasgow; Edinburgh's museums and galleries; Victorian industry in **New Lanark's** historic streets and Viking graffiti at **Maeshowe** on Orkney.

Whether you're coming just for a weekend or for a whole week, this Top 10 guide is designed to bring together the best of everything Scotland has to offer, from mysterious **Rosslyn Chapel** to mighty **Edinburgh Castle**. It provides useful tips throughout, from seeking out what's free to avoiding the madding crowds, plus 11 easy-to-follow itineraries that link a clutch of superlative sights. Add inspiring photography and detailed maps to the mix, and you have the essential pocket-sized travel companion. **Enjoy the book, and enjoy Scotland.**

Clockwise from top: **Portree harbour, Skye; Scottish dancers; Greyfriars Bobby, Edinburgh; Rua Reidh Lighthouse, near Gairloch on the northwest coast; Falkirk Wheel; Highland cattle; Scottish Parliament, Edinburgh**

Exploring Scotland

Scotland boasts wild landscapes, ancient castles and bustling cities. To help make the most of your stay and get a flavour for this fascinating country, here are ideas for a two-day and a seven-day Scottish jaunt.

The Queen's Gallery, at the Palace of Holyroodhouse, exhibits works from the Royal Collection.

Forth Bridge, a UNESCO World Heritage Site, is a cantilever railway bridge near Edinburgh.

Key
— Two-day itinerary
— Seven-day itinerary

Two Days in Scotland

Day ❶
MORNING
Start in Edinburgh with the historic **Royal Mile** *(see pp14–15)* and tour the **Palace of Holyroodhouse** *(see p15)*.
AFTERNOON
Choose between the **National Museum of Scotland** *(see pp18–19)* or the **Scottish National Gallery** *(see pp16–17)*. Wander to elegant New Town to shop at **Jenners** *(see p79)*, then take in the fabulous city views from **Calton Hill** *(see p76)*.

Day ❷
MORNING
Drive to romantic **Linlithgow Palace** *(see p86)*, then continue to the site of the battle of **Bannockburn** *(see p103)*.
AFTERNOON
Take in dramatic **Stirling Castle** *(see p103)* and the monument to William Wallace *(see p103)*. Return via the charming streets of **Culross** *(see p91)* and majestic **Forth Bridge** *(see p94)*.

Seven Days in Scotland

Day ❶
As day 1 of Two Days in Scotland.

Day ❷
MORNING
Cross the Forth to visit historic **Scone Palace** *(see p92)* before lunching by the silvery Tay in **Perth** *(see p92)*.
AFTERNOON
Head for Loch of the Lowes, near **Dunkeld** *(see p94)*, to view the ospreys (Apr–Aug). Then continue through Pitlochry to the picturesque gorge at **Killiecrankie** *(see p94)*.

Day ❸
MORNING
Ride the UK's highest funicular railway up **Cairngorm** *(see p35)*, then warm your cockles at a distillery on Speyside's **Malt Whisky Trail** *(see p35)*.

Map labels:
Dunvegan Castle
Kyle of Lochalsh
Eilean Donan Castle
Loch Coruisk
Elgol
Skye
Aug
Armadale
Mallaig
Glenfinnan
Gle
L..
Lor..
All..
Culzea..
Cas..

Eilean Donan Castle is one of Scotland's iconic sites, located on an island where three lochs converge.

AFTERNOON
Spot Moray Firth dolphins (see p112) from the shore of Spey Bay. Overnight in Highlands city **Inverness** (see p117).

Day ❹
MORNING
Explore bleak **Culloden Battlefield** (see p117), then keep your eyes peeled on a "monster" cruise on **Loch Ness** (see p117).
AFTERNOON
Watch boats on the Caledonian canal at **Fort Augustus** (see p29). Bear west to **Eilean Donan Castle** (see p118), then cross the bridge from Kyle of Lochalsh to **Skye** (see pp26–7).

Day ❺
MORNING
Start early and visit **Dunvegan Castle** (see p26), ancestral home of the Clan Macleod and purportedly the oldest inhabited castle of Scotland.

AFTERNOON
Take a boat trip from Elgol to **Loch Coruisk** (see p26). Leave the Isle of Skye from **Armadale** (see p26) in time to catch the last ferry to Mallaig (6:40pm in summer).

Day ❻
MORNING
Admire the **Glenfinnan Monument** and viaduct (see p118), and continue to sombre **Glencoe** (see pp30–31).
AFTERNOON
Take the High Road to **Loch Lomond** (see p103), stopping in pretty Luss for a break, and arriving in **Glasgow** (see pp96–101) in time for dinner.

Day ❼
MORNING
Spend the morning at **Kelvingrove Art Gallery and Museum** (see pp20–21) or the **Riverside Museum** (see p98).
AFTERNOON
Down the Ayrshire coast find **Culzean Castle** (see pp32–3) and Alloway, birthplace of Robert Burns (see p85).

Top 10 Scotland Highlights

Rib-vaulted ceiling and stained-glass windows
of St Giles' Cathedral, Edinburgh

TOP 10 Scotland Highlights

Scotland has an overwhelming abundance of natural beauty; hundreds of castles stand proud from its long and turbulent past, and an innate flair for enterprise and travel has endowed the nation with artistic treasures from around the world. The culture remains vibrant today, and there's much to celebrate. Here's a distillation of Scotland's best.

Edinburgh Castle ①

Presiding over the nation's capital, the castle is Scotland's pre-eminent sight, a truly inspirational historical and cultural landmark (see pp12–13).

② Scottish National Gallery

The gallery's internationally significant collection ranges from early Renaissance masterpieces to works by Rembrandt, Ramsay and Raeburn (see pp16–17).

③ National Museum of Scotland

The main museum has one of Scotland's great eclectic collections. The modern wing takes on Scotland from prehistory to the 20th century (see pp18–19).

Kelvingrove Art Gallery and Museum ④

Inside its grand Spanish Baroque-style shell, Scotland's premier museum and art gallery houses one of Europe's great civic art collections (see pp20–21).

⑤ Riverside Museum

This is one of Glasgow's major museums, and has a spellbinding array of interactive exhibits, visual enthralment and stimulation aplenty across all things transport and leisure. Impossible not to be wowed (see pp22–3).

Port of Ness
Kinlochbe
Stornoway
Seisiadar
Sco
Isle of Lewis
The Minch
Le
Tarbert
Gairloch
Uig
Shieldaig
Dunvegan
Raasay
Isle of Skye ⑥
Broadford
Elgol
Loch Morar
Mallaig
Fort Wil
Coll
Kilchoan
Glenco
Tiree
Dervaig
Scarnish
Isle of Mull
Ob
Iona
Inver
Atlantic Ocean
Kilmartin
Jura
Port Askaig
Tarbert
Islay
Du
Portnahaven
Port Ellen
Gigha
Ar
Campbeltown
Culze
North Channel
Ca
Cairn
Dru

6 Isle of Skye

Skye is an island of romantic tales and the pursuit of royalty, of strange landscapes and formidable mountain ranges, of castle strongholds and religious communities *(see pp26–7)*.

Loch Ness and the Great Glen 7

The Great Glen is Scotland's deepest cut, a swath that splits the land in two. A course of water runs through this great valley, forming notorious Loch Ness *(see pp28–9)*.

8 Glencoe

Described by Dickens as the "burial ground of a race of giants", there is indeed something ominous about this raw terrain, site of a 1692 massacre *(see pp30–31)*.

9 Culzean Castle

The castle stands proud on a windswept clifftop, but Culzean is a velvet hand in an iron glove; inside is given over to Robert Adam's play on the rules of Classicism *(see pp32–3)*.

The Cairngorms 10

This region offers truly spectacular views. Bird lovers, walkers and winter sports enthusiasts praying for snow all head to the woodlands, rivers, lochs and mountains of the Cairngorms, the highest landmass in Great Britain. From ospreys to Arctic flowers, it's all here to discover *(see pp34–5)*.

🔟⭐ Edinburgh Castle

Dominating the city's skyline since the 12th century, this castle is a national icon and, deservedly, the country's most popular visitor attraction. Din Eidyn, "the stronghold of Eidyn", from which Edinburgh takes its name, was the vital possession in Scotland's wars. Varying roles as royal palace, barracks, prison and parliament have all helped shape this castle, home to the Scottish crown jewels and the fabled Stone of Destiny.

① Gatehouse and Portcullis Gate

The gatehouse was built in 1886–8 more for its looks than functionality. The two bronze statues are of William Wallace and Robert the Bruce (see pp102–3). The original entrance was via the formidable Portcullis Gate of around 1574.

② Great Hall

The outstanding feature of this hall (below) is the hammer-beam roof supported on projecting stone corbels. Take time to study all the enchanting little carvings. Constructed around 1500, this is Scotland's oldest wooden roof and probably its most magnificent.

Edinburgh Castle

③ Argyle Battery

The castle's northern defence offers spectacular views. Don't miss the One O'Clock Gun, fired here every day except Sunday from a great 25-pounder cannon.

④ Crown Jewels and the Stone of Destiny

The UK's oldest crown jewels have lain here since about 1615. However, the fabled Stone of Destiny has been here only since 1996 (see box).

⑤ Scottish National War Memorial

The National War Memorial (right) lists all of Scotland's war dead since 1914. Exterior carvings include a phoenix, symbol of the surviving spirit.

7 St Margaret's Chapel

This tiny, charmingly simple building is the oldest structure surviving from the medieval castle. Probably built by David I (1124–53) in honour of his sanctified mother, it is still used today, and contains some wonderful stained glass **(left)**.

8 Royal Palace

Here in 1566, in a small panelled chamber, Mary Queen of Scots gave birth to James VI, the first king to rule both Scotland and England.

9 Governor's House

An elegant and beautifully proportioned house. It can only be viewed from the outside, as it is still reserved for ceremonial use.

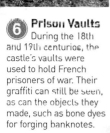

10 Mons Meg

A cannon of awesome proportions **(below)** now sits outside St Margaret's Chapel. Built in Belgium in 1449, it could fire a 150-kg (330 lb) stone ball over 2 miles (3.5 km) – cutting-edge technology in the Middle Ages.

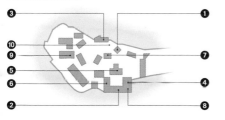

6 Prison Vaults

During the 18th and 19th centuries, the castle's vaults were used to hold French prisoners of war. Their graffiti can still be seen, as can the objects they made, such as bone dyes for forging banknotes.

Plan of the Castle

STONE OF DESTINY

According to the mythology that surrounds the Stone, this is the very rock that Jacob used as a pillow when he dreamed of angels ascending to heaven (Genesis 28). For centuries it was kept in Scone Palace, near Perth *(see p92)*, and used as the coronation throne for Scottish kings until Edward I invaded in 1296 and carried the Stone back to England. For 700 years it was kept under the throne in Westminster Abbey, until it was returned to Scotland in 1996.

NEED TO KNOW

MAP M4 ■ Castle Hill, Edinburgh, EH1 2NG
■ (0131) 225 9846
■ www.edinburghcastle.gov.uk

Open 1 Apr–30 Sep: 9:30am–6pm daily; 1 Oct–31 Mar: 9:30am–5pm daily; last adm 1 hour before closing
■ Closed Christmas Day & Boxing Day ■ Tours every 30 min

Adm £16.50; concessions £13.20; children £9.90

■ The official tours are wonderful, witty and informative. You can also take a multilingual audio tour, proceeding in whatever order takes your fancy.

■ Although a large variety of food can be found on the Royal Mile just outside the castle, choice at the castle itself is limited to either the Queen Anne Café or the Redcoat Café.

🔟 The Royal Mile

John Knox's House on Edinburgh's Royal Mile

① John Knox's House
**MAP P3 ■ 43–5 High St
■ (0131) 556 9579 ■ www.
tracscotland.org ■ 10am–6pm Mon–
Sat (also Jul & Aug: noon–6pm Sun)
■ No disabled access ■ Adm**

The best-known little house in
Edinburgh, with its quaint steps up
from the street, is now part of the
Scottish Storytelling Centre. It was
the home of Scotland's fiery religious
reformer, John Knox, in 1599. Worth
squeezing into for its antiquity alone.

② Writers' Museum
**MAP N3 ■ Lady Stair's Close
■ (0131) 529 4901 ■ www.edinburgh
museums.org.uk ■ 10am–5pm Mon–
Sat (also Aug: noon–5pm Sun)**

Occupying Lady Stair's House (built
in 1622) and set in a charming
courtyard, this is the place to learn
about the three great Scottish
writers, Robert Burns, Sir Walter
Scott and Robert Louis Stevenson,
through portraits, manuscripts and
personal possessions.

③ St Giles' Cathedral
**MAP N4 ■ High St ■ (0131) 225
9442 ■ www.stgilescathedral.org.uk
■ May–Sep: 9am–7pm Mon–Fri,
9am–5pm Sat, 1–5pm Sun; Oct–Apr:
5pm closing every day ■ Donation**

This building has been a landmark
and a marvel since 1160. Look for
the bagpiping angel (near entrance),
the exhilarating rib-vaulted ceiling
of the Thistle Chapel and those
ancient tatty flags. Lower Aisle is
a restaurant on the premises.

④ Scottish Storytelling Centre
**MAP P3 ■ 43–5 High St ■ (0131)
556 9579 ■ www.tracscotland.org/
scottish-storytelling-centre
■ 10am–6pm Mon–Sat**

A theatre with a wide range of
entertainment, but the insider thing
to do here is enquire about the local
storytellers. They hold meetings in
the Waverley Bar on the last Friday
of every month, where anyone can
enjoy the *craic* (good yarns). Nothing
flamboyant, but real local culture.

THE ROYAL MILE

The city's most historic street formed
the main thoroughfare of medieval
Edinburgh, linking the castle to
Holyroodhouse. It buzzes with charm
and surprises. Congested with street
performers during the Festival *(see
p70)*, it is a hub of activity and
entertainment year-round. Don't miss
the narrow closes off the main street.

5 Museum of Childhood
MAP P3 ■ 42 High St ■ (0131) 529 4142 ■ www.edinburgh museums.org.uk ■ 10am–5pm Mon–Sat, noon–5pm Sun

Teddy bears, rocking horses, toy soldiers and castor oil – childhood memories come rippling back in the minds of adult visitors. But today's children find the Museum of Childhood just as enthralling, to see what amused the "oldies" long ago.

6 Historic and Ghostly Tours
(0131) 225 5445; www.mercattours.com ■ (0131) 557 4700; www.auldreekietours.com ■ (0131) 225 6745; www.witcherytours.com

A fascinating tour can be taken of Mary King's Close, a medieval street sealed up in 1646 after its inhabitants died of the plague. Alternatively, choose an adrenalin-pumping ghost tour – evenings are best. Enlightening and fun.

The Witchery Tour

7 Scottish Parliament
MAP R3 ■ (0131) 348 5200 ■ www.scottish.parliament.uk ■ 9am–6:30pm Tue–Thu; 10am–5pm Mon, Fri, Sat, public hols & all days Parliament is in recess

Spanish architect Enric Mirralles's controversial design of "upturned boats" won the competition for a landmark building for the new Scottish Parliament. Higher up the Mile is the old Parliament House.

8 Museum of Edinburgh
MAP Q3 ■ 142 Canongate ■ (0131) 529 4143 ■ www.edinburgh museums.org.uk ■ 10am–5pm Mon–Sat (also Aug: noon–5pm Sun) ■ Only partial disabled access

The Museum of Edinburgh is a medieval house with a specialist local collection. A maze of rooms comprises primitive axe heads, Roman coins and all manner of historical finds gathered from the street since the Neolithic Age.

9 The Palace of Holyroodhouse
MAP R3 ■ (0131) 556 5100 ■ www.royalcollection.org.uk ■ Apr–Oct: 9:30am–6pm daily; Nov–Mar: 9:30am–4:30pm daily; last adm 1 hour before closing ■ Closes irregularly, so check in advance ■ Adm

The royal residence best known for love and murder in the time of Mary Queen of Scots. The state rooms are still used by the current Queen. Climb nearby Arthur's Seat in Holyrood Park for sensational views.

10 Camera Obscura
MAP M4 ■ Castlehill ■ (0131) 226 3709 ■ www.camera-obscura.co.uk ■ Apr–Jun: 9:30am–7pm daily; Jul & Aug: 9am–9pm daily; Sep & Oct: 9:30am–7pm daily; Nov–Mar: 10am–6pm daily ■ Adm

This historic observatory has a roving mirror that projects a 360° panorama of Edinburgh, so it is a great place to start exploring the city. It also drops you into a world of illusion and warped images to startling effect.

Camera Obscura

TOP 10 ⭐ Scottish National Gallery

A striking Neo-Classical building midway along Edinburgh's Princes Street, the National Gallery defies you to miss it and is widely regarded as one of the finest smaller galleries in the world. The collection is a manageable concentration of excellence, including works by the greatest names in Western art – Raphael, Titian, El Greco, Rembrandt, Rubens and Monet, to name but a few – as well as the most comprehensive array of Scottish masterpieces. While some galleries tend to intimidate, this one is refreshingly intimate.

1 Seven Sacraments
The seven works depicting the rites of Christianity evoke grand theatricality; they are considered the finest pieces by Nicolas Poussin, founder of French Classical painting.

2 An Old Woman Cooking Eggs
Velázquez's creation of mood through strong contrast was unprecedented in Spain when he produced this startling work in 1618 **(below)**.

3 Lady Agnew of Lochnaw
The lady's languid pose and direct gaze in this portrait **(above)** caused a stir in 1892, launching her as a society beauty and giving John Singer Sargent cult status among Edwardian-era portrait painters.

4 The Virgin Adoring the Sleeping Christ Child
The painting's brilliant range of tones has now been revealed following careful restoration. An unusual Botticelli work for having been painted on canvas and not wood.

5 Rev Robert Walker Skating on Duddingston Loch
One of the most celebrated paintings by a Scottish painter, the fun-loving minister depicted by Henry Raeburn is believed to have been a member of the prestigious Edinburgh Skating Club.

6 Dutch Portraits
The pick of the best from the Dutch collection must include Rembrandt's world-weary *Self-Portrait Aged 51*, though *A Woman in Bed* also has an impressive depth of character. The Dutch Portraits gallery also includes works by Frans Hals, including his lively, naturalistic *Portrait of François Wouters*.

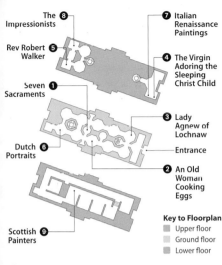

- **8** The Impressionists
- **5** Rev Robert Walker
- **1** Seven Sacraments
- **6** Dutch Portraits
- **9** Scottish Painters
- **7** Italian Renaissance Paintings
- **4** The Virgin Adoring the Sleeping Christ Child
- **3** Lady Agnew of Lochnaw
- Entrance
- **2** An Old Woman Cooking Eggs

Key to Floorplan
- Upper floor
- Ground floor
- Lower floor

THE DUKE OF SUTHERLAND

Donations in the 20th century saw the museum blossom, especially when, in 1945, the Duke of Sutherland presented the gallery with five Titians, two Raphaels, a Rembrandt and Poussin's *Seven Sacraments*. The works avoided war damage in London, having already survived the storm of the French Revolution while in the collection of the Duc d'Orleans.

7 Italian Renaissance Paintings

Works by Leonardo da Vinci and Raphael stand out here. Leonardo's drawing, *Studies of a Dog's Paw*, shows his ability to convey an entire world with just a few clever strokes, while Raphael's *Bridgewater Madonna* is alive with tenderness.

8 The Impressionists

Of the two Monets on display, *A Seascape, Shipping by Moonlight* **(below)** is a rare palette knife and brush application, while *Poplars on the Epte* is vintage Monet. Degas' *A Group of Dancers* also features

9 Scottish Painters

The collection includes superb portraits by Ramsay, Raeburn and Guthrie, *Pitlessie Fair* by Sir David Wilkie aged 16, and *Autumn in Glencairn* by James Paterson. This area is closed in 2017 for restoration.

10 Playfair's Building

William Playfair chose a Neo-Classical style to link Old and New Edinburgh. He also built the neighbouring Royal Scottish Academy and the two buildings have been joined.

NEED TO KNOW

MAP M3 ▪ The Mound, Edinburgh, EH2 2EL
▪ (0131) 624 6200
▪ www.nationalgalleries.org

Open 10am–5pm Fri–Wed (to 6pm in Aug), 10am–7pm Thu

Free except for special exhibitions

▪ For food, try the Scottish Café & Restaurant in the basement of the gallery. Decorated with handcrafted oak furniture, it takes pride in its Scottish food, offering dishes such as cullen skink, a rich smoked haddock soup. Great high tea, too.

🔟 ⭐ National Museum of Scotland

The best and rarest of Scotland's antiquities have been brought together in this treasure trove occupying adjacent buildings on Edinburgh's Chambers Street. Both buildings maintain separate identities: the older 19th-century building concentrates on international artifacts, while the modern sandstone wing is dedicated to the story of Scotland and its people.

1 Lewis Chessmen

These enchanting ivory figures – an anxious king, a pious bishop, glum warriors – were made by Viking invaders in the 12th century.

2 Monymusk Reliquary

Reliquaries were containers for storing holy relics. This one is linked to St Columba and Robert the Bruce, hero of Bannockburn (see p38). It dates back to the 8th century and, although it's tiny, the craftsmanship is exceptional. It is one of the museum's most prized possessions.

Grand Gallery, National Museum of Scotland

3 The Maiden

A grisly relic to put a shiver down your spine. The Maiden was a Scottish beheading machine, similar to the French guillotine, with a weighted blade that descended from on high. It was used to behead more than 150 condemned souls in Edinburgh between 1564 and 1710.

4 St Fillan's Crozier Head

Serving as a badge of office, this curved handle was once mounted on a staff carried by St Fillan, a 7th-century Irish monk, active in Perthshire. The filigree ornamentation exemplifies the level of artistry flourishing 1,200 years ago.

5 Bonnie Prince Charlie's Canteen

The Prince's cutlery, corkscrew, bottles, cup and condiments set. Picture the fugitive (see p27) in the wild with this lustrous travelling canteen.

6 Natural History

Dinosaur skeletons and stuffed animals **(left)** cascade down from the ceiling, producing spectacular visual results that almost bring them to life.

7 Dolly the Sheep

An unremarkable-looking sheep **(left)** that's anything but. As the world's first cloned mammal, Dolly was a scientific marvel.

8 The Buildings

The National Museum first opened as the Royal Museum in 1866 and has been a city landmark ever since. Its cavernous interior and marvellous roof create an extraordinary feeling of light and space. The sandstone wing **(right)** has been heralded as one of the most important constructions in post-war Scotland.

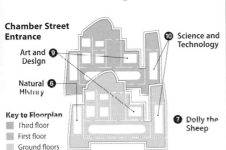

Tower Entrance

- Bonnie Prince Charlie's Canteen ❺
- Lewis Chessman ❶
- Monymusk Reliquary ❷
- St Fillan's Crozier Head ❹
- The Maiden ❸

Chamber Street Entrance

- Art and Design ❾
- Natural History ❻
- Science and Technology ❿
- Dolly the Sheep ❼

Key to Floorplan
- ■ Third floor
- ■ First floor
- ■ Ground floors

ORIENTATION

Centred on the vast foyer, the older part of the National Museum is spread over three floors. Wandering the many halls can be confusing, and some exhibits move, so pick up a floor plan. The layout of the sandstone wing – directly accessed by the Tower Entrance – is more straightforward. Exhibits are displayed in chronological order, from levels 1 to 6.

NEED TO KNOW

MAP N4 ■ Chambers St, Edinburgh, EH1 1JF ■ (0300) 123 6789 ■ www.nms.ac.uk

Open 10am–5pm daily

■ There are free guided tours daily – check at the main desk for the next tour time.

■ The museum's rooftop Tower Restaurant has fantastic views.

■ Pop around the corner to The Elephant House at 21 George IV Bridge for a coffee.

9 Art and Design

Opened in 2016, this gallery showcases innovation in applied arts, fashion and design. Among the hundreds of exhibits, the most eye-catching are six Wedgwood plates by Sir Eduardo Paolozzi from the 1970s and a flamboyant coat by Zandra Rhodes (1969).

10 Science and Technology

Dolly (see above) is just one of Scotland's modern scientific achievements. This gallery looks at some of the country's other genetic research along with its Nobel Prize-winning work on pharmaceuticals. One particularly futuristic exhibit looks at the production of state-of-the-art body implants and prosthetic limbs, developed by local company Touch Bionics.

🔟 ⭐ Kelvingrove Art Gallery and Museum

Scotland's most visited collection comprises some 8,000 works of international significance. The collection takes in worldwide ancient cultures, as well as European and Scottish art across the centuries, and provides insights into the development of Glasgow from medieval times through to its cultural transformation in the 19th to 21st centuries, including the 2014 Commonwealth Games, when the city stole the show with its hospitality and sense of fun. There is also a quirky playfulness in Kelingrove's contrasting displays.

1 Miss Cranston's Tearoom

Between 1900 and 1921 the venerable Charles Rennie Mackintosh (1868–1928) was the sole designer for Catherine Cranston's tearoom empire. These beautiful interiors are of both artistic and social significance.

2 Ceremonial Turtle Posts

These striking posts were sent to Glasgow from the Torres Straits Islands, off Australia, by a Scottish missionary in 1889 and are the only surviving examples in the world. Decorated with feathers and carvings, they conjure up mystical Islander celebrations.

West Court, Kelvingrove Art Gallery and Museum

3 Spitfire

The Spitfire LA198, 602 City of Glasgow Squadron, hangs dramatically from the ceiling of the West Court **(above)**, soaring above the bodies of stuffed giraffes and wild cats. It is recognized as the best-restored warplane of its kind in the UK.

4 Old Willie the Village Worthy

James Guthrie (1859–1930) was a leading figure in the group of young, rebellious Scottish artists known as the Glasgow Boys, who produced internationally significant work in the late 19th century. The unsentimental *Old Willie the Village Worthy* **(left)**, is one of Guthrie's finest realist portraits.

5 A Man in Armour

This fine painting by Rembrandt, considered by many the greatest artist of the Dutch Golden Age, is a bold depiction of a young man, probably Alexander the Great, weighed down by his armour. Kelvingrove curators voted it their favourite piece. The work dates back to the mid-17th century.

6 Paddle Canoe

This fascinating paddle canoe, which was carved from a single piece of wood, is one of the few remaining artifacts from a forgotten world. It dates back to Scotland's Bronze Age (c.2500–800 BC) and would have been used by early people living in crannogs, or loch dwellings.

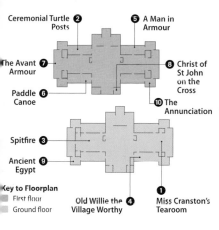

Ceremonial Turtle **2** Posts

5 A Man in Armour

The Avant **7** Armour

8 Christ of St John on the Cross

Paddle **6** Canoe

10 The Annunciation

Spitfire **3**

Ancient **9** Egypt

Key to Floorplan
First floor
Ground floor

Old Willie the **4** Village Worthy

Miss Cranston's **1** Tearoom

7 The Avant Armour

This artwork and tool of war is one of the oldest near-complete suits of armour in the world and is still in almost perfect condition. Made in Milan, a centre of armour-making, in around 1440, it is a key piece in Kelvingrove's collection.

8 Christ of St John on the Cross

Salvador Dalí's surrealist painting was first displayed in 1952. With its unusual angle of the Crucifixion, it demands attention. It has attracted admiration, criticism and controversy. Very Dalí.

9 Ancient Egypt

Egyptian wonders abound in the Ancient Egypt gallery, including the obligatory mummies and tombs. The coffin and mummy of Egyptian lady Ankhesnefer date back to 610 BC. Her mummified body has remained undisturbed since her funeral and burial approximately 2,500 years ago.

10 The Annunciation

This intimate work **(left)** by Italian master painter Sandro Botticelli (1445–1510) was probably commissioned for a private patron and used for prayer and meditation. The fine detail in the work is embellished with the use of real gold for rays of light, representing God's grace.

 **Riverside Museum**

This stunning £74 million museum sits on the banks of the Clyde and is devoted to transport and leisure. Its 3,000 fascinating items range from horse-drawn vehicles and police cars to Stanley Spencer murals and skateboards. There's a dress that was worn by Audrey Hepburn and the motorbike Ewan McGregor rode around the world. Climb aboard a tram or stand on the footplate of an historic locomotive. There are interactive displays, films and images and, moored on the quay, a 19th-century sailing ship.

1 Recreated Streets

There are three recreated streets that take you back to the Glasgow of the past. Most atmospheric is the cobbled 19th-century street with its shops, pub and an interactive photographer's studio.

2 Clyde-Built Ships

Glasgow was once a world-famous centre of shipbuilding and the museum has 159 superb models of Clyde-built ships, including luxury liners and warships. Models include the *Cutty Sark*, the *Lusitania* and the *Queen Mary*. There is also a World War I warship decorated with distinctive "dazzle" camouflage.

3 South African Locomotive

Built in Glasgow in 1945, this enormous locomotive spent over 40 years crossing South Africa. It is the largest object in the collection and one of a number of restored trains.

4 The Building

Take time after your visit to stroll around outside and take in award-winning Iraqi architect Zaha Hadid's stunning building **(left)**, which sits on the Clyde on the site of a former shipyard. The jagged roof is striking, while the interior is free of supports to accommodate the many large exhibits.

5 All Things Bike

Bicycles and motorbikes on display include Danny MacAskill's stunt bicycle, homemade bikes – and the world's oldest pedal bike. Suspended from the ceiling is a model velodrome **(above)**.

THE CLYDE

"Glasgow made the Clyde and the Clyde made Glasgow." After trade in sugar and tobacco expanded in the 18th century, engineers deepened the Clyde, which eventually allowed boats to dock in the city itself, rather than unload their cargoes downriver. International trade flourished, shipbuilding became a major industry and Glasgow grew into the "second city" of the British empire.

Glasgow Tram 6

Glasgow's trams achieved iconic status and were an important part of the city's culture until 1962. You can step inside this original streetcar **(right)** and discover stories associated with the trams and city life.

7 The Italian Café

Glasgow's Italian community has been well established in the city since the 19th century. As well as making great ice cream, they founded a number of much-loved cafés in the city and along the Ayrshire coast. Step inside this re-created 1930s café to experience those halcyon days.

NEED TO KNOW

MAP U3 ■ 100 Pointhouse Place, Glasgow G3 8RS ■ (0141) 287 2720 ■ www.glasgowlife.org.uk/museums/riverside

Open 10am–5pm Mon–Thu & Sat, 11am–5pm Fri & Sun

The Tall Ship: Pointhouse Quay; (0141) 357 3699; Feb–Oct: 10am–5pm; Nov–Jan: 10am–4pm

■ The café on the ground floor has great views of the Clyde; in warmer weather you can dine outside on the terrace.

■ There are free guided tours on most days and fun family quiz sheets. Ask at the reception.

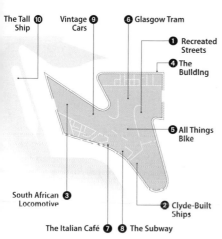

The Tall Ship 10   Vintage Cars 9   6 Glasgow Tram

1 Recreated Streets

4 The Building

5 All Things Bike

South African Locomotive 3

2 Clyde-Built Ships

The Italian Café 7   8 The Subway

10 The Tall Ship

Moored on the Clyde outside the museum, the *Glenlee* **(below)** is one of only five Clyde-built sailing ships that remain afloat. Built in the 19th century, she circumnavigated the globe four times. Go on board and tour the ship; you can even see the captain's cabin.

8 The Subway

Step into a model section of the Glasgow subway and climb into a carriage from an old underground train. You can watch a World War II drama unfold, with evacuated children and soldiers boarding the trains.

9 Vintage Cars

There aren't many places where you can see the first Hillman Imp, an Argyll motor and a pristine Strathclyde Police Ford Granada. A wide variety of old and new cars are on display **(left)**. Many are reminders of Glasgow's motor industry.

TOP 10 ★ Isle of Skye

The product of violent geographical upheavals, the "Misty Isle" is justly famed for its towering, ragged mountains and wild coastline. Add to these a colourful patchwork of crofts (farms), waterfalls, an exceptional whisky distillery, a castle linked to the fairy-tale world and the historical romance of Bonnie Prince Charlie, and you find on Skye all the ingredients that best symbolize the Scottish Highlands.

Quiraing and the Old Man of Storr (4)

A fantastic region of cliffs and pinnacles, one rocky outcrop gaining the name the Old Man of Storr (right).

(5) The Cuillins

This awesome range rises straight out of the sea to almost 1,000 m (3,300 ft). The Black Cuillins are a challenge even to seasoned climbers, but the Red Cuillins are an easier prospect for walkers.

(1) Loch Coruisk

The boat from Elgol passes seal colonies to reach this lovely loch (above), trapped in a bowl beneath the Cuillins – a prized view awaits.

(2) Aros Centre, Portree

An exceptional visitor and arts centre, created by locals with a passion for their culture. The place to learn about Skye's history and places to visit.

(6) Armadale Castle Gardens and Museum of the Isles

Beautiful coastal gardens surrounding the ruined castle of Clan MacDonald, with an historical archive.

(7) Dunvegan Castle

Dunvegan (left) was home to the chiefs of Clan MacLeod for 1,000 years. Find the Fairy Flag, which, it is said, can rally the "little people" to protect the clan.

Portree (3)

Portree is Skye's mini capital, with some excellent shops and a delightful harbour lined by colourful buildings (right). Sailing races and Highland Games are big events in summer.

Previous pages Quiraing, Isle of Skye

FLORA MACDONALD

"Bonnie Prince Charlie" was pursued relentlessly by government troops following his defeat at Culloden. He escaped to Skye disguised as maidservant to the courageous Flora MacDonald. She was imprisoned for this act. On her release she emigrated to America, but later returned to Skye, where she died in 1790, one of the prince's bedsheets her burial shroud.

⑩ Skye Museum of Island Life

Delightfully evocative, this reconstruction of thatched cottages **(below)**, or "blackhouses" (blackened by fire smoke), turns back the years a century or more.

⑧ Talisker Distillery

The so-called "lava of the Cuillins" is produced at Skye's only whisky distillery, where visitors are welcomed onto a friendly tour.

⑨ Island of Raasay

Its beauty often overlooked, Raasay offers land-based activities and watersports at its Outdoor Centre, or you can climb Dun Caan, the highest point on the island, for stunning views.

NEED TO KNOW

MAP D2

Aros Centre: (01478) 613750. www.aros.co.uk

Talisker Distillery, Carbost: (01478) 614308. Apr–Oct: 9:30am–5pm Mon–Sat (also Jun–Sep: 10am–4:30pm Sun); Nov–Mar: 10am–4:30pm Mon–Fri. Tour £8

Dunvegan Castle: (01470) 521206. Apr mid-Oct: daily. Adm £11

Misty Isle Boat Trips, Elgol: (01471) 866288

Armadale Castle: (01471) 844305. Apr–Oct: daily. Adm £9

Skye Museum of Island Life: (01470) 552206. www.skyemuseum.co.uk

Easter–Oct: Mon–Sat. Adm adults £2.50, concessions £2, children 50p

■ The Aros Centre has evenings of Gaelic culture with great local talent.

■ The Sligachan Hotel, 5 km (3 miles) west of Sconser, does great bar meals – good atmosphere and a play area for kids.

TOP10 ⭐ Loch Ness and the Great Glen

A geological rift once split the land from coast to coast, dividing Scotland in two. Glaciers deepened the trench and the result today is a long glen of steep-sided, wooded mountains and dark, mysterious lochs. Castles and forts abound, bearing witness to the Great Glen's strategic importance and enhancing its dramatic grandeur with intrigue and nostalgia. And the legendary Loch Ness Monster, elusive but irrepressible, still attracts scientific interest.

1 Caledonian Canal

The canal **(below)** is an outstanding feat of engineering by Thomas Telford, connecting lochs Ness, Oich, Lochy and Linnhe. Watch boats glide past at Fort Augustus.

2 Loch Lochy

A path on this loch's **(below)** northern shore is now part of the Great Glen Walk and cycleway. Look out for the wonderful Cia Aig waterfall on the road to Loch Arkaig.

3 Fort William

Close to Glencoe and at the foot of Britain's highest mountain, Ben Nevis (1,344 m / 4,408 ft), this seaside town provides an ideal base for walkers. Almost every direction offers enticing terrain. The less active can scale Aonach Mor on the Nevis Range ski gondola or take the Jacobite Steam Train to Mallaig.

4 Great Glen Water Park

A sensitively landscaped centre among trees on Loch Oich, the smallest and most secluded in the glen. With Monster Activities you can sail, windsurf, canoe, water-ski or shoot the rapids on a raft.

5 Glen Affric

A lovely forest road leads to this renowned beauty spot. From here, a two-day hike can take you to the west coast.

TALES OF NESSIE

First recorded by St Aiden in the 7th century, "Nessie" pops up time and again. Despite many hoaxes and faked photographs, there's still a body of sonar and photographic evidence to support the existence of large creatures here, and scientific opinion remains open. To decide for yourself, visit one of the Loch Ness Monster information centres in Drumnadrochit, which present the evidence.

6 Inverness

The "Capital of the Highlands", Inverness is a bustling shopping centre set below a pink Victorian castle. The battlefield of Culloden is nearby and the visitor centre there revives this sad and poignant event *(see p38)*.

7 Urquhart Castle

Magnificently situated on the edge of Loch Ness, these ruins **(below)** were formerly one of Scotland's largest castles. A fine tower house still stands, and the views from the top are well worth the climb. The visitor centre is state-of-the-art and displays an array of medieval artifacts.

8 Fort George

Built in the aftermath of Culloden on a sandy promontory in the Moray Firth, Fort George **(below)** is the mightiest artillery fortification in Britain. It is still in use as a barracks today, yet remarkably has only ever undergone minor modifications.

9 Loch Ness

Almost 230 m (750 ft) deep and 37 km (23 miles) long, Loch Ness is Scotland's largest body of water. Flanked by mountains, castle and abbey ruins, and several charming villages, Loch Ness is worthy of its fame. Jacobite lake cruises start from the north road along its bank.

NEED TO KNOW

MAP E3–D4

Jacobite Steam Train: (0844) 850 4685. Mid-May–Oct: Mon–Fri (mid-Jun–mid-Sep: daily)

Urquhart Castle: (01456) 450551. **Open** daily. Adm adults £8.50, concessions £6.80, children £5.10

Jacobite Cruises (Canal and Loch Ness): (01463) 233999. **Open** daily

Loch Ness Centre and Exhibition, Drumnadrochit: (01456) 450573. **Open** daily. Adm £7.45

Fort George: (01667) 460232. **Open** daily. Adm adults £8.90, concessions £7.20, children £5.40

■ The best way to see Loch Ness is by boat. Regular cruises leave from Inverness.

■ The Lock Inn (see *p119*) has decent food.

10 Fort Augustus

Fort Augustus is a delightful village situated on Loch Ness. Take a fading-sunlit, romantic evening walk in the grounds of the former abbey-school built in grand style in 1878.

TOP 10 ★ Glencoe

Nowhere else is the traveller confronted so abruptly by the arresting impact of Scotland's mountains. The road twists below the towering bulk of these characterful peaks, sometimes dark and louring, sometimes light and enticing. This ancient and celebrated pass is also imbued with history: cattle rustling, clan feuds and – most notoriously – the "Massacre of Glencoe" in 1692. In summer the area is a favourite haunt of walkers and climbers; in winter it is one of the leading ski resorts in the country.

1 Glencoe Visitor Centre

This centre possesses a superb exhibition and audiovisual presentation – allow an hour to take it all in. A satellite weather report for the area is regularly updated; useful for walkers.

THE MASSACRE OF GLENCOE

Having signed an oath of submission to William III in 1692, albeit five days late, the MacDonald clan generously entertained and billeted 130 government soldiers in their homes for 10 days. The soldiers then slaughtered their hosts, leaving 38 dead. As much as the brutality of the massacre, it was the utter breach of trust that shocked the nation.

2 Signal Rock, Glencoe Memorial and Forest Walk

A series of forest trails leads to the Signal Rock lookout (left), where the MacDonalds would light fires to send messages to other clan members.

3 Invercoe Loch Walk and Pap of Glencoe

A particularly beautiful loch (above), especially in May, when its rhododendrons are in full bloom. Behind looms the distinctive Pap of Glencoe peak, affording panoramic views.

4 Views of the Three Sisters

By a bend in the main road and next to a roaring waterfall, visitors will find a rocky knoll known as "The Study", which is a fine viewpoint for this trio of similarly profiled sibling mountains (below).

10 Glencoe Ski Centre

Among the most popular of Scotland's five ski resorts (below). All the gear is available for hire in winter, and the terrain is ideal for snow thrills.

7 Rannoch Moor

A beautiful but boggy wilderness, best seen from a window on the Fort William to Tyndrum train.

8 Scottish Sealife & Marine Sanctuary

The sanctuary's rescued seals can be seen through underwater windows, and many other sea creatures can be viewed in the aquarium. But best of all is the skate and ray pond, where you can touch these tame and elegant swimmers as they glide about.

5 Castle Stalker

A dreamlike castle, alas not open to visitors but still magical to see, rising from an island that seems barely big enough to contain it (below).

6 Loch Leven

The charming drive round this loch is punctuated by modest villages. Discover Glencoe's diverting museum and Kinlochleven's year-round ice-climbing facility, Ice Factor.

9 Devil's Staircase

A tortuous section of the West Highland Way walk (see p48), offering views to Rannoch Moor and Black Mount. The footpath continues to Kinlochleven for an even greater challenge.

NEED TO KNOW

MAP E3

Glencoe Visitor Centre:
(0844) 493 2222. www.
glencoe-nts.org.uk. Jan–
late Mar. 10am–4pm
Thu–Sun; late Mar–Dec:
9:30am–5:30pm daily
(to 4pm Nov & Dec).
Adm £6.50

Glencoe Ski Centre:
(01855) 851226. www.
glencoemountain.co.uk.
Ski day pass £32 (Jan–Apr);
chairlift £10 (Jul & Aug)

Scottish Sealife & Marine Sanctuary: (01631)
720386. www.seal
sanctuary.co.uk. Daily.
Adm £13.20

Glencoe Folk Museum:
(01855) 811664. www.
glencoemuseum.com.
Daily. Adm £3

Ice Factor: (01855)
831100. www.ice-factor.
co.uk. Daily

▪ Drive the scenic road that runs parallel to the A82 from Glencoe to the Clachaig Inn.

▪ The craft shop in Glencoe has a good menu including delicious desserts.

🔟 ⭐ Culzean Castle

Formerly a rather dull fortified tower house, Culzean (pronounced "Cullane") was transformed by the architect Robert Adam into a mansion of sumptuous proportions and elegance. The work began in 1777 and lasted almost 20 years, the Kennedy family sparing little expense in the decoration and craftsmanship of their clifftop home. Culzean – a masterpiece in a land full of magnificent castles – was gifted to the nation and fully restored in the 1970s. Its grounds became Scotland's first public country park in 1969.

3 Oval Staircase
Nothing short of perfection **(left)**. Ionic and Corinthian capitals swirl above a Georgian-patterned carpet, lit up by an arched skylight.

4 Home Farm Visitor Centre
No ordinary farm, but more of a fortified village within the country park; now it is a visitor centre and restaurant.

1 Country Park
Reckoned to be the most magnificent park in Britain, this coastal swath of woodland, ponds, gardens, beaches and clifftop walks retains the Country Park's original character **(right)**.

2 Lord Cassilis' Rooms
The restored late 18th-century decor includes vivacious Chinese-style wallpaper and a late Chippendale four-poster bed.

5 Round Drawing Room
The most beautiful room in the castle, with its circle of windows overlooking the sea.

6 Armoury
Over 1,000 weapons cover the walls in concentric patterns. The fearsome arsenal includes the largest collection of used flintlock pistols in Europe **(above)**.

ROBERT ADAM

Born in Kinross-shire in 1728, Robert Adam was educated at Edinburgh University. His subsequent tour of Italy determined his Neo-Classical style, and he went on to set up an architectural practice in London, becoming the foremost designer of his day. A true workaholic, his fanaticism for detail was legendary. Adam died in 1792, the year Culzean was completed.

7 Clifftop and Shoreline Trails

The views to the mountains of Arran are glorious from these trails. Two favourite destinations are Swan Pond and Happy Valley. Occasional free tours depart from the visitor centre, or go it alone.

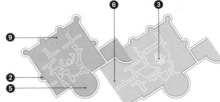

Key to Floorplan
- Ground floor
- First floor

8 Eisenhower Apartment

The apartment on the top floor was a gift to the US president for his support in World War II. It is now a small hotel **(below)**.

Culzean Castle and gardens

9 Long Drawing Room

Formerly the High Hall of the old tower house, this was the first room Adam transformed, and it was the first to be restored in the 1970s.

10 Camellia House

This impressive Gothic greenhouse **(below)** is one of more than 40 lesser architectural features found dotted around the grounds. It was designed in 1818 by James Donaldson, a pupil of Robert Adam.

NEED TO KNOW

MAP G3 ▪ Maybole ▪ (0844) 493 2148 ▪ www.nts.org.uk

Open Apr–Oct: 10:30am–5pm daily; Nov–Mar: shops & restaurant only, 11am–4pm daily; Castle grounds: 9am–sunset daily

Adm (castle) adults £15.50; concessions £11.50; family £38; one-parent family £30

▪ It's all too easy to overlook half of the Walled Garden, and so miss the wonderful Victorian Vinery, where period species of dessert grapes are grown under glass.

🔟⭐ The Cairngorms

The highest mountain massif in the British Isles comprises a magnificent range of peaks, wild lochs and ancient forests, as well as bird sanctuaries, nature reserves and sports amenities. It is a region of exceptional scenery and habitats untouched by the road network. Activities take place on its fringe, but the heartland is open only to those who travel by foot or on skis. Its relative isolation makes it appealing for the wildlife that inhabits the region and for the people who thrive on the testing terrain.

1 Aviemore
Traditionally a dormitory town for skiers as well as the jumping-off point for touring the region at any time of the year, Aviemore consists of a concentration of hotels, guesthouses, bars, restaurants and après-ski (or, indeed, après-anything) entertainment.

SPIRIT OF SPEYSIDE WHISKY FESTIVAL
A merry May festival in which you can view illicit stills and the Customs and Excise Contraband Caravan, ride The Whisky Train, dance a Highland Fling and cook your own scones against the clock. The highlight is the opulent whisky dinner set to the sounds of pipe bands.

2 Loch Morlich
Surrounded by the Caledonian pines of Rothiemurchus Forest, Loch Morlich (above) is a vast, tranquil lake at the base of the Cairngorms.

3 Loch an Eilean
Loch an Eilean is a hidden gem, 8 km (5 miles) from Aviemore. One of Scotland's best short walks is along this loch, nestling below the mountains. The trees are magnificent, and its crowning glory is an ivy-clad castle on an island.

5 Highland Wildlife Park
The once-common bison, bears and wolves may no longer roam in the wild, but you can find them here, along with otters, pine martens and wild cats (below).

4 River Spey
Scotland's finest salmon river and birthplace of whisky, the Spey (left) is a river of dark pools and fast rapids. It winds through a variety of landscapes: moorland, forest, pasture and grain field.

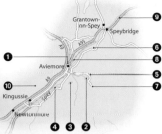

9 Malt Whisky Trail

The process of turning water into the "water of life" is a vital part of Scottish history and culture. Half of the nation's malt whisky distilleries are on Speyside, and the signposted "whisky trail" leads the way to seven of them **(above)**.

10 Cairngorm Reindeer Centre

Britain's only herd of wild reindeer **(right)** was introduced to Scotland in the 1960s. These charming animals, now numbering 150, roam free and are very friendly.

6 Loch Garten Osprey Centre

Ospreys began breeding here in 1954. More than 2 million visitors have now seen them from this hide. Vigilance has been necessary to foil egg-collectors.

7 Cairngorm Mountain Railway

This railway takes you almost to the top of Cairn Gorm mountain. The views are sublime, and at the Ptarmigan Restaurant & Bar you can enjoy the highest meal in the country.

8 Strathspey Steam Railway

The train **(below)** chuffs from Aviemore to Broomhill through a lovely landscape. On weekends there's a special Thomas the Tank Engine.

NEED TO KNOW

MAP D4–5

Highland Wildlife Park: (01540) 651270. www.highlandwildlifepark.org.uk. Daily. Adm £13

Cairngorm Reindeer Centre: (01479) 861228. www.cairngormreindeer.co.uk. Daily: Guided hill visits 11am (2:30pm May–Sep). Adm £3.50 and £13 for tours

Cairngorm Mountain Railway: (01479) 861261. www.cairngormmountain.org. Daily. Adm £11.50

Strathspey Steam Railway: (01479) 810725. www.strathspeyrailway.net. Mar–Oct. Return £14.25

Loch Garten Osprey Centre: (01479) 831476. Apr–Aug daily. Adm adults £5

Spirit of Speyside Whisky Festival: www.spiritofspeyside.com. Late Apr

Malt Whisky Trail: www.maltwhiskytrail.com

The Top 10
of Everything

**The Forth Rail Bridge, spanning
the Firth of Forth near Edinburgh**

🔟 Moments in History

St Columba

1 St Columba Founds a Monastery on Iona

In 563 this fiery Irish missionary went into self-imposed exile on Iona (known as the "home of Christianity" in Europe), and here he founded a monastery. Columban monks travelled widely, consolidating the Christian faith and thus unifying Scotland's tribes into one nation.

2 Battle of Bannockburn

Facing an English onslaught in 1314, the Scots – led by Robert the Bruce – achieved a dazzling victory. By defeating the English, the Scots won back their nation and their pride. Their right to independence was ratified by papal bull in 1329, though the war with England continued for another 300 years.

Robert the Bruce

3 Battle of Flodden

To assist France, James IV invaded England in 1513 and met the enemy just over the border at Flodden. In the massacre that followed, some 10,000 Scots died, James included, and, as his heir was still an infant, a power struggle and an era of instability ensued.

4 John Knox Leads the Reformation

Scotland was a Catholic country when Mary Queen of Scots ascended the throne. But in 1559, a revolutionary preacher called John Knox denounced Catholicism and heralded the Reformation. Protestantism was introduced to Scotland, and for the next 150 years religious intolerance was rife.

5 Union with England

When Elizabeth I died without an heir, James VI of Scotland succeeded her. He became James I of England in 1603, thus uniting the crowns. After Scotland was bankrupted by the disastrous Darien expedition, which failed to establish a colony in Panama, union with England became an economic necessity. The 1707 Act of Union united the Scottish and English parliaments, effectively dissolving Scottish Parliament.

6 Battle of Culloden

In 1745, James VII's grandson "Bonnie Prince Charlie" secretly sailed from France to Scotland to reclaim the British throne. He amassed an army which fought its way to a panic-stricken London. Short of their goal, the "Jacobites" returned north. The Hanoverian army, aided by royalist Scots, slaughtered the rebels at Culloden, the last battle fought on British soil.

7 Industrial Revolution

James Watt's transformation of the steam engine heralded the advent of the Industrial Revolution, which had a profound effect on

Glasgow in particular. The demand for steam forced every coalmine into maximum output, and the production of cotton, linen, steel and machinery boomed. Glasgow became known as "the workshop of the Empire".

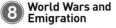

Joseph Black visiting James Watt

8 World Wars and Emigration

Of the two world wars, it was the 1914–18 war that claimed the most lives: 74,000 Scottish soldiers and almost as many civilians. In addition to this, between 1901 and 1961, 1.4 million Scots emigrated to seek better lives elsewhere.

9 Return of a Scottish Parliament

In a 1997 referendum, the Scots emphatically voted to re-establish a Scottish Parliament. This opened in 1999, returning the political forum to the heart of Scotland after an absence of 292 years.

10 SNP Gains

Scotland voted against independence in 2014, but the Scottish National Party (SNP) achieved an unprecedented result in the 2015 UK election, gaining 56 out of the 59 seats in Scotland; these MPs now sit in the UK Parliament at Westminster.

Nicola Sturgeon, leader of the SNP

TOP 10 WRITERS

J K Rowling

1 John Barbour (c. 1316–96)
The "father of Scottish poetry", wrote the epic poem *The Brus* in 1370.

2 Robert Burns (1759–96)
The famously nationalistic poet achieved a worldwide acclaim that titled him "the bard of humanity".

3 Sir Walter Scott (1771–1832)
The first best-selling author, whose novels and poems launched a romantic tradition.

4 Robert Louis Stevenson (1850–94)
Best remembered for *Treasure Island*, this revered Edinburgh author travelled widely and died in Samoa.

5 Sir Arthur Conan Doyle (1859–1930)
Mastermind behind the Sherlock Holmes novels. He was born in Edinburgh and trained as a doctor.

6 J M Barrie (1860–1937)
Born in Kirriemuir, this novelist and dramatist established his reputation with the ever-popular *Peter Pan*.

7 Hugh MacDiarmid (1892–1978)
A Drunk Man Looks at the Thistle is considered the finest poem by the "pioneer of the Scottish Renaissance".

8 Iain Banks (1954–2013)
Hugely popular author of *The Crow Road*, and other psychological thrillers and science fiction.

9 Irvine Welsh (1961–)
Best-selling cult author of street culture in Scotland. Made his mark in 1993 with *Trainspotting*.

10 J K Rowling (1965–)
This global publishing phenomenon lived in Edinburgh when she launched the *Harry Potter* series.

TOP 10 Highland Traditions

Traditional Scottish tartan kilts

1 Kilts and Tartans

The oldest tartan is dated at around AD 245. No one knows why Highlanders adopted this mode of dress or exactly when clans adopted a family "pattern" or tartan. The 1746 Dress Act banned the wearing of Highland Dress, including tartan, in a purge on Highland culture. Today, with over 2,000 registered designs, tartans are flourishing.

2 Bagpipes

No sound is more evocative of Scotland than that of the bagpipes. The great Highland pipes, dating back to at least the 14th century, are played by pipe and drum bands, and by individuals playing for competitions or dances. Over the last three decades bagpipes have emerged onto the stage of world music.

Bagpipes

3 Common Ridings

Also known as the Riding of the Marches, this ritual dates back to the Middle Ages, when young men from the Border towns (such as Hawick) would ride out to check the boundaries of the town's common land. Each town has its own version of the Riding ceremony: the oldest is the Selkirk Gathering. The Ridings, some of the oldest equestrian events in the world, take place in early summer and may last several days.

4 Gaelic Language

The rich language of the Gael can be seen on road signs and heard in shops in the Highlands and Islands. There are estimated to be 60,000 Gaelic-speakers in the country, their stronghold being the Western Isles, but even here it's a second language. Despite the increase in Gaelic education and the success of Gaelic musicians, such as Runrig, the country's youth appear less dedicated to the language and its use is in decline.

5 Curling

This sport – rather like bowls on ice – is the one in which the Scots usually excel at the Winter Olympics. Heavy circular granite stones are used, with a flat base and a handle on top. The curler slides the stone down the rink towards a bull's-eye, and team-mates, armed with brushes, polish the path ahead of the stone if more momentum is needed.

6 Shinty

This sport makes football look dull. A sort of anarchic hockey, this fast-moving game is terrific entertainment (it does have rules, but they're not apparent to the casual observer). Games take place during winter and spring in the Highlands, culminating in the Camanachd Cup Final, the nearest thing to a re-enactment of Culloden.

7 Highland Games

These are great summer spectacles that take place in communities across the land. Most popular are the kilted strongmen in the "heavy events", which include hurling monstrous hammers and tossing the caber. This is a tree trunk that must be lifted vertically, carried at a trot and tossed so that it turns end over end. Packed with bagpipes, dancers and athletes, these games are an essential part of any visit.

8 Scottish Dancing

Vital ingredients of any Highland Games are the kilted dancers competing on stage. Among

Highland dancers

the most common Highland dances are the Sword Dances, which are performed over crossed blades, and the Highland Fling. Look out too for demonstrations of the ancient tradition of step dancing, now being revived. Highland dancing is performed by solo dancers, whereas Scottish country dancing is a social dance and looks very different.

9 Sabbatarianism

Sunday is still strictly observed as a day of rest in the Western Isles. On Harris and Lewis, for instance, most local people will attend church (with unique Gaelic psalm singing); museums, attractions and public parks close; and some B&Bs will not take visitors. A limited ferry service does now exist, but it's a good idea to plan your trip ahead of time.

10 Ceilidhs

Ceilidh ("cay-lee") is a Gaelic word for a visit among friends, but it has taken on the meaning of "a party". Sometimes it is just that, a hall with a band where everyone dances. At other times it is a communal performance where people do a turn singing, dancing or playing an instrument. They are great fun and even ceilidhs held in the smallest of village halls can see turns from world-class local or touring performers.

The caber toss, Highland Games

🔟 Castles

1 Edinburgh Castle
The greatest castle in a land that's full of them, not only prized for its crowning position in the capital's heart, but also for its important history and the national treasures it holds (see pp12–13).

2 Culzean Castle
Architect Robert Adam's masterful design and exquisite taste reached their apotheosis in this castle, which ranks as one of Britain's finest mansions. Set in a park that does it ample justice, it commands a dramatic coastal position, looking seaward from the top of an Ayrshire cliff (see pp32–3).

3 Caerlaverock Castle
A triangular ruin with immense towers, Caerlaverock still sits within a filled moat. Its history spans a siege by King Edward I in 1300 and a luxurious upgrading shortly before its fall in 1640. Its yellow sandstone walls glow beautifully pink and orange in the afternoon light (see p88).

4 Stirling Castle
Dramatically perched on crags overlooking the plains where some of Scotland's most decisive battles took place, this castle was one of the nation's greatest strongholds and a key player in her history. The gatehouse, Great Hall and the Renaissance Royal Palace are outstanding. Check out the

Glamis Castle

castle's programme of special events, from tapestry weaving to sword fights (see p103).

5 Glamis Castle
MAP E5 ■ Glamis, Angus ■ (01307) 840393 ■ www.glamis-castle.co.uk ■ Apr–Oct: noon–6pm ■ Adm

This 17th-century fairy-tale castle is best known for its literary associations: Duncan's Hall provided the setting for the king's murder in Shakespeare's *Macbeth*. It also has a famous secret chamber and was the childhood home of the late Queen Mother. Rooms represent different periods of history and contain fine collections of armour, furnishings and tapestries. The gardens were laid out by 18th-century landscape gardener "Capability" Brown.

Eilean Donan Castle, on an island in Loch Duich

6 Balmoral

Queen Victoria purchased the Balmoral Estate in 1852 and transformed the existing castle into this imposing mansion set in spectacular grounds. Balmoral is still the private holiday home of the British royal family, and provides an insight into contemporary stately living *(see p110)*.

7 Dunnottar Castle

A glorious ruin on a clifftop in Aberdeenshire with the sea crashing below, this is one of Scotland's most evocative sights. In the 17th century, the Scottish crown jewels were hidden here, away from Oliver Cromwell's marauding forces. The most scenic way to arrive at the castle is by the coastal footpath from Stonehaven *(see p109)*.

8 Cawdor Castle

Whether or not the real Macbeth lived here in the 11th century, Cawdor is the sort of make-believe castle come to life to satisfy all your Shakespearean expectations. The castle is utterly magical, with its original keep (1454), a drawbridge, ancient yew tree and enough weapons to start an uprising. The garden and estate are equally enchanting and there's even a maze to get lost in *(see p111)*.

9 Eilean Donan Castle

One of Scotland's most photographed castles because of its incredible setting – huddled on an island off the shores of Loch Duich and connected to the mainland by footbridge. This 13th-century stronghold of the Clan Macrae was left to ruin until its restoration in the 1930s *(see p118)*.

10 Blair Castle

Seat of the Duke of Atholl, the only man in Britain still allowed a private army, this stately white castle is an arresting sight off the A9, the main road north. The oldest part dates from 1269, but after damage during the Jacobite campaigns Blair Castle was completely restyled and all the turrets added *(see p91)*.

Drawing room, Blair Castle

🔟 Lochs

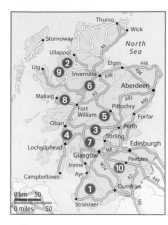

3 Loch Katrine
MAP F4

Famous as the inspiration for Sir Walter Scott's poem *Lady of the Lake*, this loch is the pearl of the area known as the Trossachs. Now incorporated into the National Park with Loch Lomond, it is sheer tranquillity compared with the other's bustle. A boat tour here is highly recommended – the SS *Sir Walter Scott* (naturally) has been doing the job for over a century.

4 Loch Awe
MAP F3

A long sliver of a loch, twisting sinuously through forested hills. The magnificent ruins of Kilchurn Castle (begun in 1440) stand at one end and testify to the stormy past of clan Campbell. Take the southern road for the best scenery, and don't be in a hurry. Close by is the defunct but preserved Bonawe Iron Foundry.

1 Loch Trool
MAP H4

An enchanting loch within a forest, in a very much overlooked corner of Scotland, characterized by its stunning wilderness. The loch is bordered by walks, which form part of the long-distance Southern Upland Way *(see p48)*. At the eastern end there's a memorial to King Robert the Bruce, King of Scots from 1306 until his death in 1329.

2 Loch Maree
MAP C3

You'll pass this loch if you visit Inverewe Gardens *(see p55)*. Wonderfully situated among imposing mountains, Loch Maree is a revered fishing location next to a nature reserve. Red deer have been known to swim out to the group of wooded islands in the centre and make temporary homes there.

Loch Awe

5 Loch Tummel
MAP E4

This small loch, with its shimmering brilliance, was a favourite of Queen Victoria, and you can stand at her

Loch Maree

Loch Tummel

legend. Forming part of Scotland's first National Park, in conjunction with the Trossachs, the loch is revered for its islands, lofty hills and shoreside leisure facilities.

(8) Loch Morar
MAP E3

The rival to Loch Ness, Loch Morar is Scotland's deepest loch at over 300 m (1,000 ft), and has long had its own legend of a monster – Morag (apparently identical to Nessie). Morar is easy to get to but little visited because its shores are largely inaccessible to cars, which makes it all the more delightful for walking. Nearby are spectacular beaches – the White Sands of Morar.

(9) Loch Torridon
MAP D3

A magnificent sea loch that is reminiscent of a Norwegian fjord. The wall of red sandstone mountains to its north attracts hill walkers, and from the summits you can see all the way from Cape Wrath to Ardnamurchan. A lovely one-way walk takes you from Diabeg to Inveralligin, with a series of refreshing lochans (small lochs) in which to swim if the weather's hot.

(10) Loch Skeen
MAP G5

The hidden treasure at the end of an utterly magical walk, Loch Skeen is a tiny loch high up in moorland hills. The walk to it climbs steeply alongside the spectacular Grey Mare's Tail waterfall (note that it's dangerous to leave the path en route). The visitor centre, situated near the falls, has a CCTV on a peregrine falcon nest.

preferred spot on the north side at Queen's View. The vista to the distant peak of Schiehallion is splendid, complemented in autumn by sweeps of colourful forest. Take the southern road to find the best picnic spots by the loch, and don't miss the river gorge walks at nearby Killiecrankie.

(6) Loch Ness
MAP D4

Probably Scotland's most charismatic loch, this deep body of water is a major draw because of the scenic splendour of the Great Glen, Urquhart Castle and the as-yet-unexplained sightings of monster Nessie *(see pp28–9)*.

(7) Loch Lomond
MAP F4

The largest surface of fresh water in Scotland, Loch Lomond's beauty is celebrated in literature, song and

🔟 Munros

1 Ben Nevis
MAP E3

Britain's highest mountain at 1,344 m (4,408 ft). A long, winding path takes you up to the top. The summit is seldom clear of cloud, but if you strike it lucky you'll enjoy unsurpassed views. In poor visibility take great care on the summit ridge as it's easy to lose the path, which borders a precipice.

Climbing Ben Nevis

2 Ben Cruachan
MAP E3

A grouping, in fact, of seven peaks overlooking lochs Awe and Etive. The highest is 1,124 m (3,688 ft) and as this summit is considerably taller than any other mountain in the area, Ben Cruachan enjoys some of the most extensive views in the country. The name "Cruachan" comes from the war cry of the Campbell clan.

3 Ben Macdui
MAP D5

Britain's second-highest mountain, at 1,309 m (4,295 ft), is best climbed from the Cairngorm ski car park. Reached by a high-altitude plateau covered in Arctic flora, it overlooks the magnificent Lairig Ghru, a deep rift dividing the Cairngorm range.

Ben Macdui

DEFINITION OF A MUNRO

Any Scottish summit over 3,000 ft (approx. 900 m) is called a "Munro" after Sir Hugh Munro, who published a list of them in 1891. There are 284 Munros, and "Munro-bagging" is a popular pastime. Most can be walked safely without climbing skills, but it is vital to plan well and be properly equipped and competent in map-reading. Conditions can deteriorate rapidly at any time of year.

4 Ben Vorlich
MAP F4

A great one to start with as there's nothing complicated about this hill, which overlooks Loch Earn, always bustling with boat activity. Take the southern road and start from Ardvorlich. At the top, at 985 m (3,232 ft), the views to the Breadalbane mountains are glorious. After drinking it in and taking some panoramic snaps, it doesn't take long to get down for tea in St Fillans.

5 Ben Lomond
MAP F4

Rising proudly from the wooded banks of its namesake loch, Ben Lomond's tall mass dominates the panorama. One of the smallest Munros at 973 m (3,192 ft), it has a well-used track, which is steep in places. There are tremendous views over the Loch Lomond and Trossachs National Park. It is best to start at Rowardennan, where there's a hotel and hostel.

6 Ben Hope
MAP B4

The most northerly Munro, with its neighbour, Foinaven. Rising starkly from the woods and moorland around Loch Hope, 927-m (3,040-ft) Ben Hope has clear views to the Orkneys. The only difficulty in bagging this peak is the scree and rocky terrain, but this is a prestigious mountain to have underfoot.

The Five Sisters, reflected in the waters of Loch Duich

⑦ The Five Sisters
MAP D3

A superb range of mountains with five prominent peaks towering above Glen Shiel in the West Highlands. Start at the highest part of the main road (A87) to save yourself an hour's climbing. Once you're on the summit ridge it's a long series of undulations, but you feel on top of the world and can see the Cuillins on Skye.

⑧ Buchaille Etive Mor
MAP E3

The 954-m- (3,129-ft) tall "Great Shepherd of Etive" stands as guardian to the eastern entrance to Glencoe. As an introduction to a place of legendary beauty, this wild mountain could not be improved. Approached from the southwest it can be climbed easily, but its magnificent crags demand respect.

⑨ Schiehallion
MAP E4

A much-loved mountain between lochs Tay and Rannoch, Schiehallion is most easily climbed from the pretty road connecting Aberfeldy with Tummel Bridge. An easy and rewarding Munro with which to launch your bagging campaign.

⑩ Liathach
MAP D3

You could pick any of the famous Torridon mountains and guarantee not to be disappointed, but this is a beauty. A massive mound of red sandstone topped with white quartzite, Liathach has distinctive parallel bands of escarpments. At 1,053 m (3,456 ft), this is a relatively difficult and strenuous mountain to climb, but worth every bit of effort.

Liathach from Loch na Frianach

🔟 Walking Routes

View from Conic Hill, West Highland Way

① West Highland Way
MAP E3–F4 ■ 150 km (95 miles)
■ 7–10 days ■ www.west-highland-way.co.uk
The first long-distance route, and still the most popular. Connecting Fort William and Glasgow, it winds past the Nevis and Glencoe ranges, crosses Rannoch Moor and skirts around every other mountain it can find. Stunning scenery, but rather close to the main road in parts.

② Southern Upland Way
MAP H3–F6 ■ 340 km (212 miles) ■ 15–20 days ■ www.southernuplandway.gov.uk
The longest walking route in Scotland, and a wonderful mix of mountain, moor, forest, loch and pasture. It crosses the country from Portpatrick in the west to Cockburnspath in the east – the preferred direction if you want the wind at your back.

③ Great Glen Way
MAP D4–E3 ■ 117 km (73 miles) ■ 4–7 days
■ www.greatglenway.com
This popular long-distance route probably packs in more dramatic scenery per mile than any other.

The walk connects Fort William with Inverness. The southern half offers easier gradients along the banks of lochs Lochy and Oich. After Fort Augustus it climbs high above Loch Ness – if that doesn't take your breath, the views will.

④ Speyside Way
MAP D4–C5 ■ 105 km (66 miles) ■ 4–6 days
■ www.speysideway.org
Bordering one of Scotland's most picturesque rivers, this path takes you from the Cairngorms to Moray's coast (with spurs to Dufftown and Tomintoul). It is a walk full of interest, with distilleries galore, bridges, stately homes and a rich abundance of wildlife.

Craigellachie Bridge, Speyside Way

5 Border Abbeys Way
MAP G5–6 ▪ 105 km (65 miles)
▪ 4–5 days ▪ www.borderabbeys way.com

Border Abbeys Way is a circular route that combines historical interest with the irresistible appeal of the gentle Borders landscape, with its rounded hills, rivers and forests. The track connects the four magnificent abbeys of Kelso, Melrose, Dryburgh and Jedburgh.

Newark Castle, Fife Coastal Path

6 Fife Coastal Path
MAP F5 ▪ 150 km (93 miles)
▪ 6–9 days ▪ www.fifecoastal path.co.uk

This walk connects the famous Forth and Tay bridges. It runs from North Queensferry, near Deep Sea World, to the small fishing villages of the East Neuk such as Elie and Anstruther, which huddle beside rugged cliffs. The route then heads north, through the historic town and golfing capital of St Andrews.

7 Cateran Trail
MAP E5 ▪ 103 km (64 miles)
▪ 5 days ▪ www.caterantrail.org

The Caterans, brigands and rustlers roamed this area in the Middle Ages. Starting in Blairgowrie's soft-fruit hills, this circular route wends to the wild mountains of Glenshee, returning via beautiful Glenisla, offering some of the best of Perthshire. This is a quieter trail than most.

WALKING ROUTES

Aside from long-distance routes, there is a vast network of local footpaths, and many areas have walking festivals. More details on walking in Scotland are available from these sites:
www.visitscotland.com
www.scotways.com
www.ramblers.org.uk/scotland
www.smc.org.uk

8 St Cuthbert's Way
MAP G5–6 ▪ 100 km (62 miles)
▪ 4 days ▪ www.stcuthbertsway.info

This is the only cross-border route in Scotland. It starts in the abbey town of Melrose and ends on the amazing island of Lindisfarne (England). It is not too strenuous a walk and a lovely mix of pasture, woodland, moor and coastal scenery. Be sure to check the tides for the last mile.

9 Cowal Way
MAP F3 ▪ 92 km (57 miles)
▪ 7 days ▪ www.cowalway.org.uk

If you like things a little wilder, try this one. The route is only partially marked, so take a good map. Start on the coast west of Glasgow at Portavadie and cross the hills of the Cowal peninsula to Inveruglas on the shores of Loch Lomond.

10 John Muir Way
MAP F4–6 ▪ 215 km (134 miles) ▪ 7 10 days
▪ www.johnmuirway.org

This route runs coast to coast, from Helensburgh in the west to Dunbar in the east. Named for John Muir, father of America's National Parks, who was born in Dunbar; his birthplace is a museum.

John Muir Way

TOP 10 Journeys

The West Highland Line crossing the River Orchy at Loch Awe

1 West Highland Line
MAP D2–F4 ■ www.westcoastrailways.co.uk

Often voted the world's most scenic railway journey, the West Highland Line runs from Glasgow to Mallaig. The journey takes around 5 hours and 30 minutes, and the train stops frequently, giving you the chance to relax and enjoy the beautiful sights of Scotland's west coast. Look out for the Glenfinnan Viaduct, which featured in the *Harry Potter* films, as well as views of Ben Nevis and Loch Eilt. If you really want to travel in style you can take the Jacobite Steam Train.

2 Take Flight

Loch Lomond Seaplanes: (01436) 675030; www.lochlomondseaplanes.com ■ Flybe: www.flybe.com

Seaplane, Loch Lomond

Soar over Loch Lomond or the Isle of Skye with Loch Lomond Seaplanes. The seaplane offers spectacular views of Scotland's lochs and mountains. Tours should be booked ahead. Another exhilarating flight is from Glasgow to Barra with Flybe. The island's runway is on a beach and disappears under the waves when the tide comes in.

3 Borders Railway
MAP F5–G5

■ www.bordersrailway.co.uk

Opened in 2015 and stretching 48 km (30 miles) between Edinburgh and Tweedbank, the Borders Railway is the longest railway line to be built in Britain for 100 years. Tweedbank station is a short walk from Abbotsford House, home of Sir Walter Scott.

4 The Road to the Isles
The A830 from Fort William to Mallaig is known as the 'Road to the Isles'. This is Bonnie Prince Charlie country and is crammed with Jacobite history. Driving it gives you the freedom to stop and explore sights, such as Glenfinnan, where Charles Edward Stuart placed his standard in 1745 and rallied the clans in his attempt to regain the crown; and Loch nan Uamh, from where he fled to France after being defeated at Culloden.

Previous pages Steam train crossing the Glenfinnan Viaduct on the West Highland Line

⑤ Steam Back in Time
www.waverleyexcursions.co.uk

A trip "doon the watter" on the PS *Waverley*, the world's last seagoing paddle steamer, is a classic Scottish journey that all ages can enjoy. Launched in 1946 and originally fuelled by coal, the ship was saved from the breaker's yard in the 1970s and is now owned by a charity. Take a summer day trip from Glasgow to destinations such as Dunoon, Rothesay and Arran. Special excursions run too.

⑥ Climb a Mountain
www.cairngormmountain.org

From the gentler slopes of the Eildon Hills in the Borders, to the mighty peak of Ben Nevis, Scotland's hills and mountains are wild, beautiful, challenging and irresistible. If you are not an experienced walker you can still enjoy the view from a mountaintop by taking the funicular railway up Cairn Gorm mountain. There's a restaurant and viewing platform at the top.

⑦ Pedal a Trail
7 Stanes Centres: www.7stanes mountainbiking.com

Whether you're a novice or an experienced biker, you're sure to find a trail to suit you in Scotland. There are demanding routes such as the Sligachan on Skye, a single-track circuit almost 45 km (28 miles) long, or gentle family-friendly trails. The 7 Stanes Centres, in Dumfries and Galloway and the Borders, offer trails to suit all abilities. They have centres at Dalbeattie, Glentrool, Ae, Kirroughtree, Mabie, Glentress and Innerleithen and Newcastleton.

Bike trail

Forth Rail Bridge

⑧ Bridge the Forth
When it opened in 1890, the Forth Bridge was the world's longest single-span cantilevered bridge. It's still an iconic structure and you'll really be able to appreciate this Victorian marvel if you take the train across it – travel from Edinburgh or South Queensferry into Fife.

⑨ Ferry Crossing
Calmac: www.calmac.co.uk ■ Argyll Ferries: www.argyllferries. co.uk ■ Skye Ferry: www.skyeferry. co.uk; operates Easter–Oct: 10am–6pm (to 7pm Jun–Aug)

Taking a ferry to a Scottish island is not just practical; it can feel wonderfully romantic. Calmac are the main operator, running services to islands such as Arran, Skye and the Inner and Outer Hebrides. Argyll Ferries run between Gourock and Dunoon and connect with trains from Glasgow Central. Loveliest of all is Scotland's last manually operated turntable ferry, the Skye Ferry, sailing between Glenelg on the mainland and Kylerhea on Skye.

⑩ North Coast 500
www.northcoast500.com

Billed as Scotland's answer to America's Route 66, the North Coast 500 is an 800-km (500-mile) circuit that will give you a real taste of the Highlands. From Inverness, the route goes west to Applecross then up the coast and along the tip of Scotland to John O'Groats, from where it heads back down to Inverness.

TOP10 Gardens

Rock garden at the Royal Botanic Garden, Edinburgh

1 Royal Botanic Garden

Edinburgh's prize garden, founded in 1670 and moved to its current site in 1820, features huge trees, rock terraces and borders bursting with colour. The glasshouses are of particular interest, containing everything from hothouse palm trees and gigantic lilies to dwarf cactuses and orchids. Watch out for special events, such as music, theatre and exhibitions of contemporary art (see also p76).

2 Dawyck Botanic Garden

MAP G5 ■ Stobo, nr Peebles ■ (01721) 760254 ■ Apr–Sep: 10am–6pm daily (to 5pm Mar & Oct, to 4pm Feb & Nov) ■ Adm

An outpost of Edinburgh's Royal Botanic Garden, where trees are the speciality. They began planting them here 300 years ago. With its enormous diversity and fine specimens, the garden is ideal for woodland walks. The visitor centre has a café, a shop and exhibitions.

3 Kailzie Gardens

MAP G5 ■ Kailzie, nr Peebles ■ (01721) 720007 ■ www. kailziegardens.com ■ Apr–Oct: 11am–5:30pm daily; Nov–Mar: daylight hours daily ■ Adm

This formal walled garden is an outstanding example of what was once more common on family estates. Marvellous roses fill the air with fragrance, and there's a pond stocked with trout for fishing.

4 Logan Botanic Garden

MAP H3 ■ Port Logan, south of Stranraer ■ (01776) 860231 ■ Mid-Mar–Oct: 10am–5pm daily ■ Adm

The Logan boasts the greatest number of exotic species growing outdoors in Scotland. The southern hemisphere is particularly well represented; the palm trees and gunnera have grown to almost jungle proportions. Apart from the climate, there's a South Pacific feel to the place. It's usually much quieter than other gardens, too.

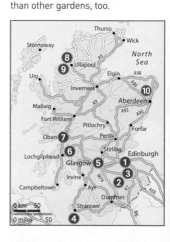

5 **Botanic Gardens, Glasgow**

Positively bulging with greenery and colour, Glasgow's Botanic Gardens are a favourite with locals and visitors alike. The magnificent gardens date from 1817, and are particularly noted for their glass-houses. Foremost among these is the curved iron framework of the restored Kibble Palace. An oasis of palm trees, ferns, orchids, begonias and many exotic species is found inside. Art exhibitions, theatre, festivals and plant shows also take place here (see also p99).

6 **Crarae Gardens**
MAP F3 ■ Nr Inveraray ■ (0844) 493 2210 ■ 9:30am–sunset daily; Visitor Centre: Apr–Oct: 10am–5pm daily (Thu–Mon in Sep & Oct) ■ Adm

A superb woodland garden with one of the country's most diverse collections of rhododendrons. Many of the seeds were gathered on private expeditions around the world and some species are now rare. In May the garden bursts into a brilliant mass of blooms (see also p104).

7 **Arduaine Gardens**
MAP F3 ■ Nr Oban ■ (0844) 493 2216 ■ 9:30am–sunset daily ■ Adm

Overlooking the sea, this garden has another famous rhododendron collection, but also includes exotic blue Tibetan poppies, giant Himalayan lilies and Chatham Island forget-me-nots. Having fallen into disrepair, Arduaine was lovingly and painstakingly restored to glory by two brothers (see also p104).

The Hydroponicum

8 **The Hydroponicum**
A totally revolutionary place, the "garden of the future" has no soil but uses a clever water irrigation system to carry nutrients to the plants. Take a tour of the growing houses where they cultivate everything from tropical flowers to bananas. You can buy your own growing kits and fresh seasonal produce (see also p120).

9 **Inverewe Gardens**
A west coast phenomenon, these much-vaunted gardens are worth travelling a long way to see. The gardens were nurtured into astonishing fertility in 1862 by Scottish aristocrat Osgood Mackenzie on his 8.5-sq-km (3-sq-mile) estate, and they became his life's work. Exotic plants, shrubs and trees from all over the world form one of the finest botanical collections in the country, all in a stunning location on Loch Ewe (see also p119).

10 **Pitmedden Garden**
Originally laid out in a Classical French style in 1675 and destroyed by a fire in 1818, Pitmedden was meticulously recreated in the 1950s. The effect is stunning. Within a vast walled area are four elaborate floral parterres, three of which have heraldic designs (see also p109).

Rhododendrons, Arduaine Gardens

⑩ Island Attractions

Skara Brae, Orkney

① Skara Brae, Orkney
The best-preserved group of prehistoric dwellings in Western Europe, this semi-subterranean village is 5,000 years old and pre-dates either the pyramids or Stonehenge. The nine houses were linked by covered passageways and you can see their "fitted" stone furniture. Artifacts such as gaming dice and jewellery are displayed in the visitor centre (see p130).

② Maeshowe, Orkney
It looks like just a grassy mound from the outside, but stoop low and walk along its narrow entrance passage and you find yourself in a stunning, 5,000-year-old chambered grave. After years of use it was closed, then rediscovered by Norse invaders – who left runic graffiti on the walls (see p130).

③ Islay's Distilleries
MAP G2/F2 ■ www.islayinfo.com
They say that Irish monks introduced distilling to Islay in the 14th century. At one time there were over 20 distilleries on the island, producing its distinctive peat-smoked whisky. Now there are just nine distilleries (with one more planned). The oldest, Bowmore, was first mentioned in 1779; the others are Ardbeg, Bruichladdich, Caol Ila, Bunnahbhain, Lagavulin, Laphroaig, Gartbreck and Kilchoman.

④ Iona Abbey and Priory
MAP F2 ■ (01681) 700512
■ Apr–Sep: 9:30am–5:30pm Mon–Sat; Oct–Mar: 9:30am–4pm Mon–Sat ■ www.historic-scotland.gov.uk, www.ionahistory.org.uk ■ Adm
Iona has been a centre of Christian worship since AD 563, when St Columba founded his monastery here. It has been a pilgrimage site for hundreds of years. St Columba's shrine can be seen, as well as the 13th-century abbey church, and 8th-century stone crosses. It is said that Scottish kings and clan chiefs were buried here.

⑤ Fingal's Cave, Staffa
MAP E2 ■ (01681) 700659
■ www.nts.org.uk
An Uamh Binn, or Cave of Melody, Fingal's Cave is a spectacular sea cave on the uninhabited island of Staffa. Its giant hexagonal columns and mystical beauty inspired Mendelssohn's *Hebrides Overture*, and featured in a painting by J M W Turner. Take a boat trip and see the island's fantastic wildlife such as basking sharks, seals and puffins.

Fingal's Cave, Staffa

6 The Italian Chapel, Orkney

MAP A5 ▪ (01856) 781268 ▪ Apr–Sep: 9am–10pm, Oct–Mar: 9am–4:30pm

Created from two Nissen huts by Domenico Chiocchetti and his fellow Italian prisoners of war between 1943 and 1944, who created this stunning little church as their memorial. Inside is trompe l'oeil brickwork and an altar made from scrap; painted glass windows depict St Francis of Assisi. Truly a labour of love.

The Italian Chapel

7 Kinloch Lodge, Skye

MAP D2 ▪ Sleat, Skye ▪ (01851) 621422 ▪ www.kinloch-lodge.co.uk ▪ £££

Lovely atmosphere at the home of Godfrey Macdonald, the chief of the Macdonald clan, and his wife Claire, an acclaimed cookery writer. Bedrooms are individually furnished, there are comfy sofas, log fires, and fine food in the restaurant. There's a cookery school, too.

8 Arran's Food Trail

MAP G3 ▪ www.visitarran.com, www.taste-of-arran.co.uk

The Isle of Arran produces a wonderful selection of food and drink. Put together your own island food trail by checking out its local oatcakes, cheeses, chocolate, whisky, beer, smoked fish, preserves and tablet (which is a bit like fudge, only harder and sweeter, see p69).

9 Callanish Standing Stones, Lewis

MAP B2 ▪ (01851) 621422 ▪ www.historic-scotland.gov.uk; www.calanaisvisitorcentre.co.uk

These magnificent stones, arranged in a cross shape with a central circle, were erected around 5,000 years ago. At a later date a chambered tomb was added. Probably built as an astronomical observatory by a religious cult, they were abandoned around 1,000 years later. There's an informative exhibition in the visitor centre (check the website for opening hours).

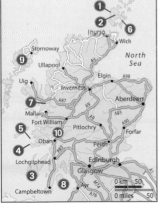

Isle of Eriska Hotel

10 Isle of Eriska Hotel

MAP E3 ▪ (01631) 720371 ▪ Apr–Oct, 2-night min ▪ www.eriska-hotel.co.uk ▪ £££

Get away from it all at this sumptuous hotel, housed in a baronial castle and located on the tiny island of Eriska. On the grounds is a golf course, a spa, a swimming pool, a Michelin-starred restaurant and lots of local wildlife. In addition to hotel rooms, there are now two self-catering lodges.

For a key to hotel price ranges see p144

🔟 Golf Courses

1 St Andrews
MAP F5 ▪ (01334) 466666
▪ www.standrews.org.uk

Every golfer dreams of playing here. There are seven courses, including, most famous of all, the Old Course. Book months in advance or take your chance in the lottery for unreserved places held the day before. Fit in a visit to the Golf Museum too. The plush restaurant at the Old Course Hotel is excellent (see p95).

Playing the Old Course, St Andrews

2 Turnberry
MAP G3 ▪ (01655) 331000
▪ www.turnberry.co.uk

Purchased by Donald Trump in 2014 and situated on the Ayrshire coast, the Ailsa Course has tested all the world's great players. Access to the Arran Course is difficult unless you stay at the hotel. For expert tuition and a review of your game, contact the Colin Montgomerie Links Golf Academy, a multi-million-pound addition to the hotel.

3 Carnoustie Championship Course
MAP E5 ▪ (01241) 802270
▪ www.carnoustiegolflinks.co.uk

A delightful course, the superb links and great character of which have earned it a world-class reputation. You'll need to present your handicap certificate to play here and reserve your tee time in advance, but there are two other good links if you don't get on the main one. Saturdays can be busy throughout the year.

4 Gullane
MAP F5 ▪ (01620) 842255
▪ www.gullanegolfclub.com

Almost every blade of grass in this corner of East Lothian is dedicated to golf. Muirfield is the elite course but a private club. Gullane No. 1 is open to anyone (handicap certificate required), while Nos. 2 and 3 have no restrictions. If Gullane is crowded, you can drive a short way to North Berwick, Haddington or Aberlady, and seven more top courses.

5 Muirfield
MAP F5 ▪ Gullane ▪ (01620) 842123 ▪ www.muirfield.org.uk

This 18-hole championship course dates back to 1891, when it was first laid out by Tom Morris. Situated in lush East Lothian, by the pretty village of Gullane, it is home to the Honourable Company of Edinburgh Golfers. Visitors' days are Tuesday and Thursday. Availability of tee times can be checked in advance.

Turnberry Hotel

Fairway bunkers on Gleneagles golf course

6 Gleneagles
MAP F4 ■ (01764) 662231
■ www.gleneagles.com

Another legendary group of courses, in beautiful moorland attached to a luxurious hotel. Queen's Course is the shortest, then comes King's and finally Monarch's, a marathon 6,475 m (7,081 yards). No handicap certificates required. Andrew Fairlie has a delectable restaurant here *(see p68 & p95)*.

7 Troon
MAP G4 ■ Old Course & Portland: (01292) 311555; www.royaltroon.com ■ Darley, Fullarton, Lochgreen, Kilmarnock: (01292) 616255; www.golfsouthayrshire.com/courses

Among the six courses there's one for everyone, from Fullarton's fun course for beginners to the classics such as Darley and Portland. But the best is the Old Course, a vintage Open venue. You need to apply well in advance.

8 Old Prestwick
MAP G4 ■ (01292) 671020
■ www.prestwickgc.co.uk

New courses come and steal the limelight but Old Prestwick glows as an enduring favourite. In 1860 it was the first venue to hold the British Open Championship. It remains a challenging course and one of Scotland's most venerated. Very busy, especially at weekends.

A golfer drives

9 Royal Dornoch
MAP C4 ■ (01862) 810219
■ www.royaldornoch.com

The Championship Course has 18 pristine holes. It was laid out by Tom Morris in 1877 and follows the natural contours of the dunes around Dornoch Bay. A wonderful setting and less pressurized than other quality links.

10 Nairn
MAP D4 ■ Nairn: (01667) 453208; www.nairngolfclub.co.uk ■ Nairn Dunbar: (01667) 452741; www.nairndunbar.com

There are two championship courses here. The Nairn hosts major tournaments but also has a nine-hole course, the Newton, for holiday golfers. Nairn Dunbar is the other top-notch course.

TOP10 Whisky Distilleries

Whisky barrels at Springbank

1 Springbank
MAP G2 ■ Cambeltown
■ (01586) 551710 ■ www.
springbankwhisky.com ■ Adm

Cambeltown was once a whisky
smuggling centre, and the
Springbank distillery, which dates
back to 1828, was built on the site
of an illicit still. This independent,
family-owned business produces
three distinctive malts – Springbank,
Longrow and Hazelburn – and offers
a choice of tours and tastings.

2 Glenlivet
MAP D5 ■ Ballindalloch
■ (01340) 821720 ■ www.the
glenlivet.com ■ Mar–Nov: 9:30am–
4pm Mon–Sat, noon–4pm Sun

One of the first distilleries to be
legalized in 1824, the Glenlivet has
been at the forefront of the industry
ever since. A comprehensive tour
includes the musty warehouse where
the whisky ages for 12 to 18 years.

3 Laphroaig
MAP G2 ■ Nr Port Ellen, Islay
■ (01496) 302418 ■ www.laphroaig.
com ■ Tours daily (Mon–Fri only in
Jan & Feb) ■ Adm

With their heavy smoked-peat
flavour, the Islay malts really are in a
class of their own. Even if you think
you won't like them, try them! This
malt is pronounced "la-froyg", but in
truth your pronunciation doesn't
matter – the taste is famous enough
for instant recognition. A delightfully
informal and intimate tour with
plenty of wit and grist at a fine
sea-edge location.

4 Talisker
MAP D2 ■ (01478) 614308
■Tours Apr–Oct: Mon–Sat (Jun–Sep:
daily); Nov–Mar: Mon–Fri ■ Adm

The only distillery on Skye and it's
been producing a highly respected
malt since 1830 (see p27). Lively,
informative tours last 40 minutes.

5 Lagavulin
MAP G2 ■ Port Ellen, Islay
■ (01496) 302749 ■ www.discovering-
distilleries.com ■ Tours Mar–Oct:
daily; Nov–Feb: Mon–Sat ■ Adm

Like its rival Laphroaig, this is a very
distinctive malt. Lagavulin whisky is
made in a traditional distillery with
unusual pear-shaped stills. The tour
here is highly personal and refreshingly free of the
feeling of mass-
market hustle.

**Lagavulin
distillery**

LAGAVULIN

Copper sills, Edradour distillery

best tour. Maybe because they're so remote, they try harder. Prepare to be taken through deep piles of malt drying in a delicious reek of peat.

9 Cardhu

MAP D5 ■ Knockando ■ (01340) 872555 ■ www.discovering-distilleries.com ■ Apr–Jun: Mon–Sat; Jul–Sep: daily; Oct–Mar: Mon–Fri ■ Adm

The only distillery to have been pioneered by a woman and, aside from producing a distinguished single malt, it provides the heart of the Johnnie Walker blend. This is one of the smaller distilleries.

6 Edradour

MAP E5 ■ Nr Pitlochry ■ (01796) 472095 ■ www.edradour. com ■ Tours mid-Apr–mid-Oct: Mon–Sat ■ Adm

Established in 1825, this is Scotland's smallest distillery and its cluster of buildings has remained virtually unchanged since the 1860s. To witness the process here is all the more delightful for its being in miniature. Only 12 casks a week are produced, making the screigh (as they say) "a rare treat for a few".

7 Glenfarclas

MAP D5 ■ Ballindalloch ■ (01807) 500345 ■ www. glenfarclas.co.uk ■ 10am–4pm Mon–Fri (Apr–Sep: to 5pm; Jul–Sep: also 10am–4pm Sat) ■ Adm

One of the few independent companies and justly proud of it. Established in 1836, this distillery is still owned and managed by the fifth generation of the Grant family. Tour the gleaming copper stills and then finish off by taking a dram in the splendid Ships Room.

8 Highland Park

MAP A5 ■ Nr Kirkwall, Orkney ■ (01856) 874619 ■ www.highland park.co.uk ■ Tours Mon–Fri (May–Aug: daily) ■ Adm

Not the most famous whisky (though definitely among the greats), but the

10 Macallan

MAP D5 ■ Craigellachie ■ (01340) 872280 ■ www. themacallan.com ■ Easter–Sep: 9:30am–6pm Mon–Sat; Oct–Easter: 9:30am–5pm Mon–Fri ■ Adm

Macallan is another of the famous Speyside brands, and the distillery boasts one of the most modern visitor centres in the valley. Aside from a guided tour, you explore whisky-making using the latest interactive technology. For an extra £15 you can become a connoisseur by prearranging an individually tutored nosing and tasting tour.

Macallan

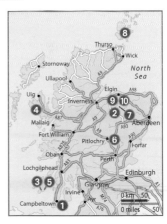

🔟 Scotland for Free

Scottish Parliament building, Edinburgh

1 Museums for Free

All city museums in Glasgow and Edinburgh are free, so you won't have to pay to see many of the country's highlights, such as the National Museum of Scotland *(see pp18–19)*, the Scottish National Gallery *(see pp16–17)* and Kelvingrove Art Gallery and Museum *(see pp20–21)*.

2 Free Festival

www.freefestival.co.uk
Don't worry if you can't afford tickets to events in the Edinburgh Festival: the city is full of street performers in August, so just stroll around and enjoy the show. There is a free fringe programme too.

3 Holy Orders

Most of Scotland's churches are free to visit, including the historic St Giles' Cathedral in Edinburgh *(see p14)* and Glasgow Cathedral *(see p97)*, though donations are welcome. The exquisite Italian Chapel *(see p57)* in Orkney is free too.

Pictish carved stone

4 Seat of Power

MAP R3 ▪ Horse Wynd
▪ Tickets: (0131) 348 5000 or 0800 092 7500 ▪ www.scottish.parliament.uk
Scotland's increasingly powerful Parliament sits in a striking (or strikingly ugly, depending on your opinion) contemporary building at the foot of Edinburgh's Royal Mile. You can visit for a free tour and even book a free ticket to attend First Minister's Question Time.

5 The Picts

MAP E5 ▪ Aberlemno
The Picts left few visible reminders of their presence in Scotland, except for their mysterious carved stones and crosses. View some for free around Aberlemno, a short drive north of Glamis.

6 Wild at Heart

St Abbs Head National Nature Reserve, Eyemouth: (01890) 771443, www.nts.org.uk
▪ Scottish Dolphin Centre, Spey Bay: (01343) 820339, www.wdcs.org, Apr–Oct: 10:30am–5pm
Scotland's wildlife is rich and varied, and it doesn't have to cost you a penny to see it. St Abbs Head National Nature Reserve is free and offers the chance to spot seabirds such as guillemots, kittiwakes and razorbills. At the Scottish Dolphin Centre you can enjoy free land-based dolphin watching, hourly from 11am to 5pm.

Stained glass, St Giles' Cathedral

7 Glorious Garden

Entry is free to Glasgow's glorious Botanic Gardens, which offer riverside walks and an arboretum, as well as stunning Victorian glasshouses, the most famous of which is the Kibble Palace. There are fascinating guided walks in the summer (see p55 & p99).

8 A Free Dram

The Glenlivet distillery near Ballinadalloch offers a free 45-minute tour of the entire whisky-making process and includes a taste of their single malt. They also have a leaflet outlining three signposted walks in the glen (see p60).

9 Ancient Trees

Scotland boasts some mighty trees that you can see for free. The most famous are the Birnam Oak in Dunkeld (see p94), said to be the last survivor of Birnam Wood mentioned in Shakespeare's *Macbeth*; and the 3,000-year-old Fortingall Yew in Fortingall's churchyard – a contender for Britain's oldest tree, a short drive west of Pitlochry (see p93).

The Birnam Oak, Dunkeld

10 Salmon Leap
MAP E4/5 ■ Pitlochry

On the Tummel in Pitlochry, you can watch salmon leaping up the specially constructed fish ladder, which bypasses a hydroelectric power station and allows thousands of fish to complete their annual migration.

TOP 10 BUDGET TIPS

Road bridge to the Isle of Skye

1 National Trust for Scotland
www.nts.org.uk
Membership provides free entry to over 100 of their properties.

2 Historic Scotland Explorer Passes
www.historic-scotland.gov.uk
For three or seven days, gives free entry to 78 properties.

3 VAT Refund
Non-EU visitors can reclaim the 20 per cent Value Added Tax (VAT) at participating stores.

4 Getting to the Isle
Use the road bridge rather than the ferry to reach Skye. It's free.

5 Freedom of Scotland Pass
www.britrail.net
A four or eight-day Freedom of Scotland Pass gives free travel on railways and many ferries.

6 Cairngorms Golf Pass
www.visitcairngorms.com
A pass provides 30 per cent off green fees at any of 12 courses.

7 Lunch It
Make lunch your main meal. Many top-tier (pricey) restaurants do great-value set menu lunches.

8 Sandemans New Europe
www.newedinburghtours.com
Sandemans offers free 2.5-hour walking tours of Edinburgh.

9 Mackintosh Trail
www.crmsociety.com
A one-day ticket (£10) covers all of Glasgow's Mackintosh sights.

10 Itison
www.itison.com
An active online market for daily deals on accommodation, restaurant meals and activities. Check regularly, or subscribe.

🔟 Attractions for Children

Go Ape treetop trail

① Go Ape
www.goape.co.uk

Zip-wire and treetop thrills in Glentress Forest, near Peebles; Crathes Castle, near Aberdeen and Queen Elizabeth Forest Park, near Loch Lomond – the last includes a 400-m (1,300-ft) zip wire over a 27-m- (90-ft-) high waterfall.

② Museum of Childhood
MAP P3 ▪ 42 High St, Edinburgh ▪ (0131) 529 4142 ▪ 10am–5pm Mon–Sat, noon–5pm Sun

A feast of nostalgia, with toys from the 18th to 21st centuries – everything from teddy bears to Teletubbies, Meccano sets to snakes and ladders, comics to satchels and slates. A real family attraction.

③ Our Dynamic Earth
MAP R3

Housed in a spiked tent, this electrifying exhibition is a mix of education and entertainment. You travel through all sorts of environments, from volcanic eruptions to the Ice Ages. Stand on shaking floors, get caught in a tropical downpour, fly over prehistoric Scottish glaciers and come face-to-face with extinct dinosaurs. The exhibition also goes further, looking at our future and pondering the realities of climate change (see also p76).

④ M&D's Scotland's Theme Park
MAP F4 ▪ Motherwell ▪ (01698) 333777 ▪ www.scotlandsthemepark.com ▪ mid-Mar–mid-Oct: phone or check website for times ▪ Adm

Huge fairground fun centre with everything that gravitational and centrifugal forces can do to you. Big wheel, free-fall machine, flying carpet, kamikaze whirligigs and the giant "500 tons of twisted fun" roller-coaster. For the younger children there are gentler water chutes and merry-go-rounds. There's also Amazonia, an indoor tropical rainforest.

⑤ Kelburn Country Centre
MAP F3 ▪ Nr Largs ▪ (01475) 568685 ▪ www.kelburnestate.com ▪ Adventure Park & Secret Forest Apr–Oct: 10am–6pm daily; Grounds: all year ▪ Adm

The family estate of the Earls of Glasgow doubles as an adventure park. The surprise-packed Secret Forest gets the best vote, and kids will go berserk in the indoor play barn and adventure play areas. Pottery workshop, spectacular displays of falconry and well-organized pony treks.

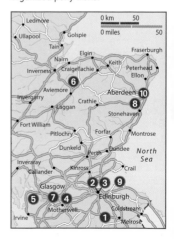

Runaway Timber Train ride at Landmark Forest Adventure Park

⑥ Landmark Forest Adventure Park

MAP D4 ■ Carrbridge, nr Aviemore ■ (0800) 731 3446 ■ www.landmark park.co.uk ■ Apr–Oct: 10am–6pm daily; Nov–Mar: 10am–5pm daily ■ Adm

A play and adventure centre based around a tree theme. Join the squirrels on the Tree Top Trail, climb the tallest timber tower in the country or ride the Runaway Timber Train. There's also a Spiderman's delight of climbing apparatus.

⑦ Glasgow Science Centre

MAP U3 ■ 50 Pacific Quay, Glasgow ■ (0141) 420 5000 ■ www.glasgowsciencecentre.org ■ Apr–Oct: 10am–5pm; Nov–Mar: 10am–3pm Wed–Fri, 10am–5pm Sat & Sun ■ Adm

Housed in a landmark building, three floors of hands-on experiments puzzle and delight with miraculous science. There's an IMAX screen and the world's first revolving tower.

⑧ The Den & The Glen

MAP D6 ■ Maryculter, nr Aberdeen ■ (01224) 732941 ■ www.denandtheglen.co.uk ■ 9:30am–5:30pm daily (last entry 4:30pm). ■ Adm

A family theme park with giant-sized models of nursery rhyme and storybook characters for kids to explore and enter make-believe worlds. Humpty Dumpty, Pooh and Postman Pat are among those present and there's a good indoor play area too: the Den.

⑨ Scottish Seabird Centre

MAP F5 ■ The Harbour, North Berwick ■ (01620) 890202 ■ www. seabird.org ■ Apr–Aug 10am–6pm daily, closes earlier rest of year ■ Adm

Interactive live cameras let you zoom in on the wildlife of the Firth of Forth islands without disturbing them. See gannets, kittiwakes, cormorants, puffins and, between October and December, grey seals with their pups. The centre also offers boat trips to the Bass Rock or Isle of May.

Gannet, Bass Rock

⑩ Beach Leisure Centre

MAP D6 ■ Beach Promenade, Aberdeen ■ (01224) 655401 ■ Daily (flume times vary) ■ Adm

Aberdeen has 10 swimming pools, but this is the one for flumes. There's a mini-flume for tots, but older children will be after the hairiest and scariest: the Pipeline, Wipeout and Tube. The last of these you ride on a tyre, while as for the other two … just close your eyes and hope for the best.

⒑ Best-Kept Secrets

Boats moored by the entrance to Morar River

① Walk from Loch Morar to Tarbet

MAP E3 ■ 20 km (12 miles); approx 6 hours ■ Book the ferry in advance: (01687) 462233

A combined walk and boat trip through sublime scenery. From Morar's silver sands, follow Britain's shortest river (half a mile) to the loch. Tarred at first, the way turns into an undulating track, which wends to its destination at the lovely bay of Tarbet. Arrive by 3:30pm to catch the ferry back to Mallaig.

② Old Forge Music Venue

MAP D3 ■ Inverie ■ (01687) 462267

The Old Forge offers legendary music sessions, open fires, superb, unpretentious food and free moorings if you arrive by boat. The sea almost laps at the door, and Knoydart's scenery is among the best. The Old Forge has been classed by the *Guinness World Records* as the most remote pub in mainland Britain.

③ Sunset from Craig Mountain Bothy

MAP C3 ■ Mountain Bothies Association: www.mountainbothies.org.uk

A simple, isolated cottage with five-star views over the sea to Skye and the Western Isles – sunsets are utterly breathtaking. Only accessible by foot, Craig is 5 km (3 miles) from

Little Diabeg or 9 km (5 miles) from Red Point – and a lovely walk it is, too. You'll need to bring all provisions and a sleeping bag, and bear in mind there's no phone on site.

④ Falls of Foyers

MAP D4

The more rain, the merrier for this one, so leave your visit until after a wet day. The upper falls are impressive; the lower falls even more so, plunging a spectacular 62 m (200 ft). The yellow-white torrent gushes into a black bowl, hollowed deep in the forest near Loch Ness, and the almighty roar of the rushing water is as awe-inspiring as the magnificent sight itself.

Falls of Foyers on the River Foyers

5 Elie Chain Walk
MAP F5

As exciting as it is short, this 2.5-km (1.5-mile) cliff walk involves steep carved steps and chains bolted into rock to allow high-tide access between the coves. The best route is to walk west along the cliffs from the small town of Elie, descend to sea level at the tip of the headland, and then return along the chain walk. The chains are inaccessible for 2 hours at high tide, and are unnecessary at low tide.

6 Knoydart
MAP D3 ■ www.knoydart-foundation.com

The most remote part of mainland Britain, this peninsula of rugged hills and glens lies in a time warp that's inaccessible by car. However, regular ferries from Mallaig provide access to the village of Inverie and outdoor activities including deer-stalking and mountain biking. Knoydart is a favourite destination for landscape photographers, which says much about its beauty.

Loch Hourn, Knoydart

7 Drive from Ullapool to Kylesku
MAP C3–B3

Scotland's most beautiful road. Drive it in spring when it's almost consumed by yellow-flowering whins, or in winter when surf erupts against the shore, or on a blue summer evening when Assynt's mountains assume the shape of absurd scribbles. But do drive it: take the A835 north from Ullapool, go west at Drumrunie, follow signs to Lochinver, then the B869 to Kylesku.

Village Bay, St Kilda

8 St Kilda
For info about visiting St Kilda, check out www.kilda.org.uk

Scotland's first World Heritage Site, this archipelago of monumental cliffs was, until 1930, inhabited by a highly individual community who lived off the islands' millions of seabirds. Such is St Kilda's isolation that it has its own subspecies of mouse, wren and sheep. Hard to get to, but if you can it'll touch your soul.

9 Sandwood Bay
MAP B3 ■ Nr Kinlochbervie

Perhaps it's the colourful strata patterning the rocks (Lewisian gneiss, among the world's oldest) or the quality of the sand. Perhaps it's the huge stack that stands sentinel at one end like some antediluvian shepherd. Or the Atlantic waves that charge in with billowing crests. Or is it the fact that so often you can have this mind-stretching expanse of beach to yourself?

10 Regional Feis
Feb–Oct ■ Feisean nan Gaidheal: (01478) 613355 ■ www.feisean.org

A feis ("faysh") is a festival of Gaelic arts combined with workshops. Lasting several days, most take place in the Highlands and islands, always with terrific performances and blistering dances.

TOP 10 Eating Experiences

Anstruther Fish Bar

1 Fish and Chips

You can't beat fresh fish and chips eaten beside the sea – and few places do it better than the award-winning Anstruther Fish Bar (www.anstrutherfishbar.co.uk) in the pretty fishing village of Anstruther in Fife. Even Prince William has been here.

2 Sample some Seafood

Argyll and the islands are noted for their excellent seafood, with restaurants serving fresh local oysters, mussels and scallops as well as lobsters and langoustine. Follow the seafood trail (www.theseafoodtrail.com).

3 Enjoy an Italian Ice Cream

Italians began migrating to Scotland in the late 19th century. Many made a living making ice cream and some of the cafes they opened are now Scottish institutions. Two of the best are Nardini's in Largs (www.nardinis.co.uk) and Luca's in Musselburgh (www.s-luca.co.uk).

4 Have a Picnic

Food always tastes better outdoors so, on a fine day, make the most of Scotland's fresh air and have a picnic. Many hotels and B&Bs will happily prepare you one, then simply head for a loch side, a deserted beach or a country park.

5 Take Afternoon Tea

Enjoyed between 3pm and 5pm, afternoon tea is served in smart hotels. Think fine china, a selection of teas, dainty sandwiches (filled with things like smoked salmon or roast beef), scones (topped with jam and cream), shortbread and cake, such as fruity Dundee cake.

6 Dine at a Michelin-Starred Restaurant

Scotland boasts several Michelin-starred restaurants: in fact there were 16 at the last count, with award holders found everywhere from Edinburgh to Nairn. For two-star dining there's Andrew Fairlie at Gleneagles (www.andrewfairlie.co.uk), while one-star establishments include Three Chimneys (threechimneys.co.uk) and Kinloch Lodge (www.kinloch-lodge.co.uk) on Skye, and The Peat Inn (www.thepeatinn.co.uk) in Fife.

Nardini's ice cream parlour

7 Try an Arbroath Smokie
The Arbroath Smokie – fresh haddock smoked over hardwood chips – is a delicacy from the coastal town of Arbroath. The Arbroath Smokie Trail lists restaurants, shops and producers where you can try this tasty traditional dish.

Tablet sign

8 Try some Tablet
No, it's not a local medicine, despite the name. Tablet is a delicious Scottish confection similar to fudge but crumblier and a great deal sweeter. It makes a novel gift and keeps for six months. You'll find it on sale everywhere.

9 Curry in Glasgow
Glasgow is Scotland's most ethnically diverse city and has a reputation for its excellent Indian food: it has frequently been proclaimed the "curry capital" of the UK. Great restaurants include Mother India (www.motherindia.co.uk) and the Ashoka Southside (www.ashokasouthside.info).

Full Scottish breakfast

10 Eat a Full Scottish Breakfast
Whether you're staying in a modest B&B or a luxurious country house hotel, have a full Scottish breakfast of bacon, eggs, tomato, mushroom, baked beans, sausage, black pudding and a potato "tattie" scone. Don't forget the porridge, of course.

TOP 10 SCOTTISH DISHES

Arbroath Smokies

1 Haggis
Scotland's most famous dish is like a large, round sausage containing spiced sheep's offal, oats and seasoning. It is traditionally eaten at a Burn's supper with mashed "neeps" (swedes), "tatties" (potatoes) and a dram of whisky.

2 Venison
The meat of wild red deer, dark and full-flavoured. It's served as a steak or cut into collops (slices of roast meat).

3 Grouse
One of Scotland's prized game birds, this dark meat is roasted and served with home-made bread sauce.

4 Stovies
A mix of potatoes, onions and beef cooked in the dripping (fat) from the Sunday roast.

5 Kippers
Fresh herring split open, salted and smoked. A common breakfast dish.

6 Arbroath Smokies
Similar to kippers, but these are smoked haddock rather than herring.

7 Smoked Salmon
Thin boneless slices of salmon that have been smoked to give a rich taste and deep pink colour.

8 Scotch Broth
A light soup made from mutton or beef stock, pearl barley and various vegetables such as carrots and leeks.

9 Cock-a-Leekie Soup
A warm, chunky soup of chicken, leeks, rice and prunes cooked in chicken stock – as wonderful as its name.

10 Cullen Skink
A Scottish version of chowder, this is a delicious soup made from smoked haddock, milk and mashed potato.

TOP 10 Cultural Events

1 Edinburgh International Festival, Fringe and Military Tattoo

Festival: Aug; (0131) 473 2000; www.eif.co.uk ▪ Fringe: 5–29 Aug (approx); (0131) 226 0026; www.edfringe.com ▪ Tattoo: 5–27 Aug (approx); (0131) 225 1188; www.edintattoo.co.uk

The greatest extravaganza of music, drama, dance and opera on the planet. The Festival features the world's most prestigious performers, while the thousand-show Fringe brings the unknown and avant-garde. The massive spectacle of the castle's Military Tattoo parade is a swelling moment of national pride and vitality – a highly charged affair.

Performer at Celtic Connections

4 Celtic Connections

Venues throughout Glasgow ▪ Mid-Jan–late Jan ▪ (0141) 353 8000 ▪ www.celticconnections.com

The world's largest festival of Celtic music and culture, with performers from as far afield as Mongolia and the Cape Verde islands, as well as the Scots and Irish.

5 Edinburgh International Film Festival

MAP L4 ▪ Filmhouse ▪ Mid-Jun–late Jun ▪ (0131) 228 2688 ▪ www.edfilmfest.org.uk

Established in 1947, the festival now comprises four categories: world premieres, young British talent, film study and a major retrospective.

6 T in the Park

MAP F5 ▪ Mid-Jul ▪ www.tinthepark.com

Sponsored by the Tennent's brewery, this is Scotland's biggest annual rock concert. The fields of Kinross are smothered in tents, while the bands get to perform in a giant castle of a marquee. Book in advance.

Edinburgh Fringe Festival

2 Glasgow Jazz Festival

End of Jun ▪ (0141) 552 3552 ▪ www.jazzfest.co.uk

A jamboree that swamps the city with devotees of jazz and supplies top international musicians. Venues range from theatres to pubs, clubs and ad hoc stages.

3 Edinburgh International Book Festival

MAP L3 ▪ Mid-Aug–late Aug (approx) ▪ (0845) 373 5888 ▪ www.edbookfest.co.uk

Charlotte Square plays host to this annual showcase of literary talent, bringing together best-selling and critically acclaimed authors for readings, debates and book signings.

7 Lanimer Day

MAP G4 ▪ Lanark ▪ Early/mid-Jun ▪ www.lanarklanimers.co.uk

Based on the annual custom of walking the town's boundaries (which started in 1140), this festival has developed into a week of fun events and fairground thrills. The highlight is the long parade of decorated floats, usually covered in thousands of paper flowers, and children dressed in outlandish costumes. A great community atmosphere prevails.

8 St Magnus Festival
MAP A5 ■ Orkney
■ Late Jun ■ (01856) 871445
■ www.stmagnusfestival.com

The Orkney islands have worked hard to create a cultural festival of exceptional quality. Events usually include at least one world premiere of either music or drama, and some of the world's best musicians. Timed to coincide with midsummer, the festival uses the remarkable island landscape to striking effect.

9 Shetland Folk Festival
Shetland ■ Early May
■ (01595) 694757
■ www.shetlandfolkfestival.com

These islands are the heartland of Scottish fiddle-playing, and this festival not only showcases the prodigious home-grown talent but also attracts the best from far afield.

10 Edinburgh International Science Festival
Early to mid-Apr ■ (0131) 553 0320
■ www.sciencefestival.co.uk

Successfully combining education with entertainment in venues right across the city. There are exhibitions of the latest scientific advances, demonstrations of tomorrow's gadgets and serious debates.

Edinburgh Science Festival

TOP 10 RIOTOUS EVENTS

Up Helly Aa, Shetland

1 Hogmanay, Edinburgh
Scotland's New Year's Eve. Crowds pack Princes Street (ticket only) and the castle is lit up by fireworks (31 Dec).

2 World Pipe Band Championships
Astonishing sights and sounds as 3,000 pipers from around the world play on Glasgow Green (mid-Aug).

3 Glasgay
One of the UK's largest gay and lesbian festivals (early Nov, Glasgow).

4 Royal Highland Show
Over 150,000 people celebrate the biggest, best and most cultivated in the farming world (Jun, Edinburgh).

5 Edinburgh International Jazz & Blues Festival
A rival to Glasgow's, this is the capital's own festival of cool music with venues across the city (late Jul/early Aug).

6 Speyfest
The best folk and traditional music performers gather at Fochabers (between Elgin and Buckie) in early August.

7 Up Helly Aa
An incredible fire festival. Men dress as Vikings and burn a replica longboat (late Jan, Shetland).

8 Burns An' A' That!
Scotland's top musical talent celebrates Scottish culture at venues around Ayrshire (late May).

9 Borders Rugby Sevens
Skill, passion and mud. In rugby's heartland, each border town takes a day as host (Apr/May).

10 The Ba', Kirkwall
Wild ball game and free-for-all played in the town's crowded streets (Kirkwall, Orkney, 1 Jan).

Scotland
Area by Area

The Dugald Stewart Monument
on top of Calton Hill, Edinburgh

⌈TOP 10⌋ Edinburgh

National Museum of Scotland

With 18 golf courses, a dozen major parks, sufficient Neo-Classical architecture to dub it "the Athens of the North" and the crowning splendour of its castle, Edinburgh ranks as one of the world's most beautiful cities. Its centre is split in two: the historic Old Town, with its cobblestones and narrow wynds (alleys); and the striking Georgian architecture of the New Town. Between them lies Princes Street Gardens, a bowl of greenery in the heart of the bustle. No other city crams in as many festivals during the year as Edinburgh, and in August it becomes the greatest showcase on earth for comedy, music, drama, dance and every other conceivable form of culture.

AREA MAP OF EDINBURGH

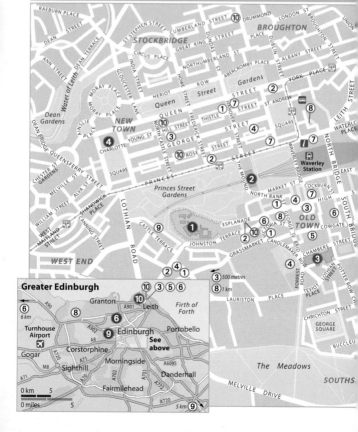

Edinburgh Castle on Castle Rock

The Royal Mile treads a straight but diverting path from the castle to Holyroodhouse (see pp12–15).

1 Edinburgh Castle and the Royal Mile

This world-famous castle wears the nation's history. Here you'll find the Scottish Crown, Sword and Sceptre, and the legendary Stone of Destiny.

2 Scottish National Gallery

Scotland's leading gallery includes masterpieces by the great Scottish artists, such as Raeburn and Ramsay, but is best known for its 15th- to 18th-century British and European paintings. In these collections, you'll find works by Botticelli, Velázquez, Raphael, Rembrandt, Rubens, Titian and many more besides (see pp16–17).

3 National Museum of Scotland

Two adjoining buildings in radically different styles and with very diverse contents present the nation's most treasured historical artifacts. Worth visiting for the Lewis Chessmen alone, but don't expect to escape in under four hours (see pp18–19).

4 Georgian House

MAP L3 ■ 7 Charlotte Square ■ (0844) 493 2118 ■ www.nts.org.uk ■ Apr–Jun, Sep & Oct: 10am–5pm; Jul & Aug: 10am–6pm; Nov & Mar: 11am–4pm ■ Adm

A restored mansion on Charlotte Square, this is the best place to start a walking tour of the New Town. The area was the first daring adventure into planned architecture at a time of sordid living conditions for the masses. Begun in 1776, the beautifully proportioned buildings, set out in wide streets, crescents and squares, have lost none of their grandeur. Simply wander.

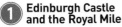

ONTGOMERY ST.

OLD PL

HILLSIDE CRESCENT

LONDON ROAD

ROYAL TERRACE

CALTON

Regent Gardens

REGENT TERRACE ROAD

REGENT

ABBEY HILL ABBEYMOUNT

CALTON ROAD

HORSE WYND

CANONGATE

HOLYROOD ROAD

CANONGATE

HOLYROOD GAIT

QUEEN'S DRIVE

COWGATE

Holyrood Park

Sailsbury Craig

PLEASANCE

DUMBIEDYKES

LEONARD'S STREET

CLERK STREET

0 metres 250
0 miles 250

1	Top 10 Sights see pp75–7
1	Places to Eat see p81
1	Bars and Pubs see p80
1	Places to Shop see p79
1	The Best of the Rest see p78

Bedroom at Georgian House

5 Our Dynamic Earth

MAP R3 ■ Holyrood Rd ■ (0131) 550 7800 ■ www.dynamic earth.co.uk ■ Apr–Oct: 10am–5:30pm daily (to 6pm in Jul & Aug); Nov–Mar: 10am–5:30pm Wed–Sun ■ Adm

Every bit as exciting and illuminating for adults as it is for kids, Our Dynamic Earth takes you on a journey through time from the Big Bang to the present. Amid this rapid evolution, environmental concerns are brought to the fore *(see also p64)*.

6 Royal Botanic Garden

MAP K5 ■ 20a Inverleith Row, Edinburgh ■ (0131) 552 7171 ■ www. rbge.org.uk ■ Mar–Sep: 10am–6pm daily (to 5pm Feb & Oct; to 4pm Nov & Jan) ■ Adm for glasshouses

Scotland's premier garden with species from around the world. The guided tours will feed a curiosity you won't have realized you had *(see p54)*.

7 Holyroodhouse

MAP R3 ■ Royal Mile ■ www.royalcollection.org.uk ■ Apr–Oct: 9:30am–6pm; Nov–Mar: 9:30am–4:30pm ■ Adm

Originally the abbey guesthouse, this was turned into a royal palace by James IV of Scotland and is the Queen's official Scottish residence; she visits each summer. The Queen's Gallery is lined with portraits of Scottish royalty. The Royal Apartments are associated with Mary, Queen of Scots: it was here that David Rizzio, her

PRINCES STREET GARDENS

An area of neutrality between New Town and Old, these lovely gardens (below) shelter under the wing of the clifftop castle. During the Festival they become a major events venue, and throughout summer the famous Floral Clock, comprising over 2,000 plants, ticks away in a corner by The Mound.

Italian secretary, was brutally murdered on the orders of her husband, Lord Darnley. The Queen meets ministers and dignitaries in the State Apartments.

8 Calton Hill

MAP P2

Rising above the New Town with fantastic views, Calton Hill is home to a gathering of Classical buildings: the columned National Monument for the dead of the Napoleonic Wars, the Nelson Monument, commemorating the Battle of Trafalgar and the Old City Observatory.

Holyroodhouse

Scottish National Gallery of Modern Art

9 Scottish National Gallery of Modern Art

MAP J3 ■ 75 Belford Rd
■ www.nationalgalleries.org
■ 10am–5pm daily (to 6pm in Aug)

Since it opened in 1960, this gallery has amassed some 5,000 post-1890 works. Here you can find the hand of such diverse figures as Picasso, Munch, Charles Rennie Mackintosh and the Pop Art trio of Richard Hamilton, David Hockney and Jake Tilson. Also check out Modern Two opposite for contemporary shows.

Royal Yacht *Britannia*

10 Royal Yacht Britannia

MAP K5 ■ Ocean Terminal, Leith ■ (0131) 555 5566 ■ www. royalyachtbritannia.co.uk ■ Apr–Oct: 9.30am–4.30pm daily; Nov–Mar: 10am–3:30pm daily ■ Adm

From 1953 to 1997 this was the Queen's floating home, the honeymooning hotel of her children and Britain's roving royal court. Wander the decks of this fabulous ship with an audio tour that tells of the life and times of *Britannia*.

A DAY IN EDINBURGH

▶ MORNING

Have a leisurely start and be at the **Scottish National Gallery** (see pp16–17) when it opens at 10am. Ninety minutes should allow you to see the Botticelli, Canova and Raeburn's skating minister, the Rev Robert Walker, as well as far more besides.

Enter **Princes Street Gardens** at the **Floral Clock** (opposite the gallery), and ascend the path to **Edinburgh Castle** (see pp12–13), taking care, as it's a steep climb.

Tour the castle, keeping an eye on your watch to make sure you're present when the One O'Clock Gun goes off – very dramatic! As you're now at the **Queen Anne Café**, have a platter to restore your energy levels before soldiering on.

AFTERNOON

Stroll down from the Castle Esplanade to the **Royal Mile** (see pp14–15), stopping off at the **High Kirk** and probably several shops as well. Admire **John Knox's House** and have hot chocolate in **The Elephant House** on George IV Bridge, where the first of the Harry Potter books was written.

Turn right off the Royal Mile at Reid's Close (easy to miss) and visit **Our Dynamic Earth**, where you can pass several million years in a mere 2 hours or so.

If you still feel energetic, walk up the Salisbury Crags and **Arthur's Seat** for spectacular evening views. Ninety minutes up and down (if you're fit) or grab a taxi and be driven most of the way up.

See map on pp74–5

The Best of the Rest

① The Writers' Museum
MAP N3 ■ Lady Stair's House, Lawnmarket ■ www.edinburgh museums.org.uk

Celebrating the lives of three great Scottish writers: Burns, Scott and Stevenson, The Writers' Museum contains rare books and items such as Burns' writing desk (see p14).

The Writers' Museum sign

② Scottish National Portrait Gallery
MAP N2 ■ Queen St ■ www.nationalgalleries.org

Marvel at over 3,000 portraits of famous Scots, including Robert Burns and Bonnie Prince Charlie.

③ St Giles' Cathedral
MAP N4 ■ High St ■ www.stgilescathedral.org.uk

It was in this 12th-century church that John Knox launched the Scottish Reformation. Attractions include the Thistle Chapel and a memorial to Robert Louis Stevenson (see p14).

④ Greyfriars Kirk
MAP N4

Historic church, best known for its statue (in the street) of "Greyfriars Bobby" (1858–72), a devoted terrier who lived by his master's grave.

⑤ Surgeons' Hall Museum
MAP P4 ■ Nicolson St ■ (0131) 527 1649 ■ www.museum.rcsed.ac.uk ■ Adm

Great for morbid curiosity, but also to appreciate Edinburgh's contribution to surgery. Sections cover midwifery, bodysnatching and war medicine, plus an exhibit on Sir Arthur Conan Doyle.

⑥ Hopetoun
MAP J5 ■ Sth Queensferry ■ (0131) 331 2451 ■ www.hopetoun.co.uk ■ Adm

This fine architectural gem, work of the industrious Robert Adam, is both a stately home and an art treasury (paintings by Canaletto, Rubens, Rembrandt, to name but a few).

⑦ Real Mary King's Close
MAP N3 ■ 2 Warriston's Cl, High St ■ (0845) 070 6240 ■ www.realmarykingsclose.com ■ Adm

Shiver as you tour this warren of streets hidden beneath the City Chambers. Closed off after the 1645 plague, they are said to be haunted.

⑧ Lauriston Castle
Davidson's Mains ■ (0131) 336 2060 ■ www.edinburghmuseums.org.uk ■ Adm

This Edwardian mansion boasts a 16th-century tower house, lovely grounds, and fine furniture and antiques. Admission by tour only.

⑨ Scottish Mining Museum
Newtongrange ■ (0131) 663 7519 ■ www.scottishminingmuseum.com ■ Adm

Don your headlamp for an enlightening underground tour.

⑩ Scotch Whisky Experience
MAP M4 ■ Castlehill ■ (0131) 220 0441 ■ www.scotchwhiskyexperience.co.uk ■ Adm

A replica distillery with the world's largest collection of Scotch whisky.

Places to Shop

1 Edinburgh Books
MAP M4 ▪ 145 West Port

One of a handful of independent bookshops just to the west of Grassmarket selling a mix of new and second-hand books. West Port's selection focuses on the arts.

2 Hector Russell
MAP M3 ▪ 95 Princes St

Made-to-measure kilts and a gathering of the tartans. Also a branch on the High Street.

3 Whistles
MAP M2 ▪ 97 George St

One of several boutique fashion stores that have made George Street their home. High fashion for women.

4 Royal Mile Whiskies
MAP N4 ▪ 379 High St

A cornucopia of all things alcoholic, particularly single malt Scotch whisky, with hundreds of varieties on offer and regular tasting sessions.

5 Printmakers' Workshop
MAP P1 ▪ 23 Union St

A range of limited-edition works from contemporary printmakers at very reasonable prices.

6 Iain Mellis
MAP N4 ▪ 30 Victoria St

Iain Mellis's cheeses are celebrated all around Scotland, and feature on many an Edinburgh menu, but the Victoria Street branch goes beyond matters dairy to embrace a panoply of culinary delicacies. Stock your picnic hamper here.

Cheeses at Iain Mellis

Jenners department store

7 Jenners
MAP N3 ▪ 47 Princes St

The oldest department store in the world, founded in the 1830s but only occupying its present site since 1895. Jenners sells a miscellany of high-quality goods, luxury brands and designers in grand surrounds.

8 Halibut & Herring
MAP L6 ▪ 108 Bruntsfield Place

Scottish handmade soaps and all manner of colourful, squeezy and curvaceous bathroom accessories in aquatic hues. A useful stop for presents to take home.

9 Edinburgh Farmers' Market
MAP L4 ▪ Castle Terrace

The city's weekly foodie fest spreads its wares beneath the castle crags every Saturday morning, selling everything from Scottish cheeses and venison sandwiches to local craft beers and traditional Scottish sweets.

10 Tiso Edinburgh
MAP M3, 123 Rose St
▪ Leith branch: 41 Commercial St

An outdoor clothing and gear shop, Tiso Edinburgh has everything you need before heading for the hills. The Leith branch also offers a café and a sports therapy clinic.

See map on pp74–5

Bars and Pubs

1 Bow Bar
MAP N4 ■ 80 West Bow St

Lush red and cream gloss paintwork envelops this modest room of a pub, where the background sounds are provided by the jovial babble of conversation and clinking glasses.

2 The Blue Blazer
MAP L5 ■ 2 Spittal St

A place for discerning drinkers, with real ales and an array of malt whiskies. The back room hosts regular live folk-music sessions.

3 Bennet's
MAP L6 ■ 8 Leven St

Ever popular, its one-time ordinary pubness rapidly becoming exotic: big old mirrors, a mix of ages, drinks in pint pots and cheap lunches.

4 Dome Bar
MAP M2 ■ 14 George St

Dome Bar is a Corinthian-columned whale of a building, entered through a flight of steps flanked by nocturnal doormen. Ballooning chandeliers, palm plants and a choice of bars: the vast and theatrical circle bar or the plush and cushioned side bar, with its evocation of the 1930s.

Lavish interior of Dome Bar

Craft beer bar, BrewDog

5 BrewDog
MAP N4 ■ 143 Cowgate

Scotland's most successful artisan brewery operates this industrial-chic altar to craft beer, a hugely popular oasis of real ales in the Old Town.

6 City Café
MAP P4 ■ 19 Blair St

Ideally situated in the heart of the city's clubland, this venerable and popular bar always packs in the capital's contingent of party people on weekend nights.

7 Bramble
MAP M2 ■ 16a Queen St

Stone steps lead down to this maze-like, candlelit cellar where accomplished mixologists create some of Edinburgh's finest cocktails.

8 Café Royal Circle Bar
MAP N2 ■ 19 West Register St

Swirling ceilings, brass lamps and a convivial atmosphere of both young and old, at lunchtime enjoying simple seafood dishes from the kitchen of the Oyster Bar next door.

9 John Pearce
MAP P1 ■ 23 Elm Row, Leith Walk

Swedish owners have taken this century-old Scottish pub and given it a Scandinavian makeover, creating a welcoming and family-friendly bar.

10 The Cumberland
MAP M1 ■ 1–3 Cumberland St

This is a much-loved pub, its lights beckoning on cold winter nights, its pleasant side garden equally coquettish in the summer heat.

Places to Eat

PRICE CATEGORIES

For a three-course meal for one with half a bottle of wine (or equivalent meal), taxes and extra charges.

£ under £30 ■ ££ £30–60 ■ £££ over £60

1 Henderson's

MAP M2 ■ 94 Hanover St ■ (0131) 225 2131 ■ ££

Delicious wholesome cafeteria food is served in a bohemian setting at this vegetarian restaurant. There is live music in the evening.

2 The Witchery by the Castle

MAP M4 ■ Castlehill ■ (0131) 225 5613 ■ ££

Aim for the Secret Garden room to experience the Witchery at its romantic best. Excels at dishes with a rural flavour: honey-roasted duck, terrines of venison and pheasant.

3 Restaurant Martin Wishart

MAP K5 ■ 54 The Shore, Leith ■ (0131) 553 3557 ■ £££

Book ahead for this Michelin-starred restaurant. The food is memorable and lunch excellent value.

4 Timberyard

MAP M4 ■ 10 Lady Lawson St ■ (0131) 221 1222 ■ ££

Authenticity and originality are the watchwords at this beautifully converted woodworking shop. The focus is on locally produced seafood, pork and game garnished with foraged ingredients, such as damsons and mustard leaf.

Pigeon ornament, Timberyard

5 Fishers, Leith

1 The Shore, Leith ■ (0131) 554 5666 ■ ££ ■ Sister restaurant, Fishers in the City, 58 Thistle St (MAP M2)

This seafood restaurant is loved for its honed cooking and warm ambience.

6 The Kitchin

MAP F5 ■ 78 Commercial St ■ (0131) 555 1755 ■ £££

Tom Kitchin's restaurant has made a startling impact on the country's culinary scene. Find out what makes this Leith outlet special by sampling some of the exemplary French-influenced cuisine.

Elegant dining area at Number One

7 Number One

MAP N3 ■ The Balmoral, 1 Princes St ■ (0131) 557 6727 ■ £££

Chef Jeff Bland serves top-notch cuisine befitting of this restaurant's setting inside one of Scotland's grandest hotels, The Balmoral.

8 Ondine

MAP N4 ■ 2 George IV Bridge ■ (0131) 226 1888 ■ ££

Seafood, from Scottish lobster to Portuguese prawns via Breton shellfish, graces the menu at this sleek and sophisticated restaurant.

9 Gardener's Cottage

MAP Q1 ■ 1 Royal Terrace Gdns, London Rd ■ (0131) 558 1221 ■ ££

Diners share communal tables in this cosy eatery, where the set menu changes daily with ingredients from the cottage's own organic garden.

10 Le Café St-Honoré

MAP M2 ■ 34 North West Thistle St Lane ■ (0131) 226 2211 ■ ££

Bistro food that's both familiar and better than ever. A charmer!

See map on pp74–5

TOP 10 Southern Scotland

A beautiful region of abrupt and rolling hills, sheep pastures, forested valleys and slow-moving rivers, Southern Scotland is the home of rugby, Robert Burns, Sir Walter Scott and spectacular castles and abbeys. For centuries this border country was the flashpoint of hostility between Scotland and England, but also a centre of commerce and religion. The monuments of these times represent some of the best medieval and Renaissance architecture in Europe. Still sparsely inhabited, the border towns contest their rugby reputations in winter and, with equal passion, celebrate ancient riding festivals in summer.

Burns Monument, Alloway

AREA MAP OF SOUTHERN SCOTLAND

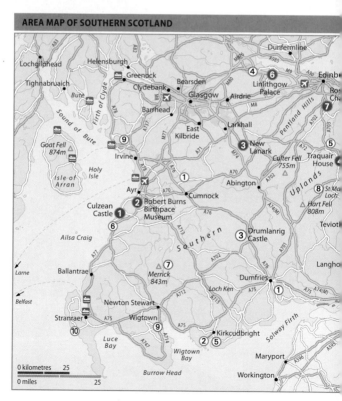

Previous pages The Falkirk Wheel at night

1 Culzean Castle

This cliff-edge castle was remodelled into a magnificent home for the Earls of Cassillis in 1777 by Georgian architectural master Robert Adam *(see pp32–3)*.

2 Robert Burns Birthplace Museum

MAP G4 ■ Murdoch's Lone, Alloway ■ (0844) 493 2601 ■ www.burns museum.org.uk ■ Apr–Sep: 10am–5:30pm (to 5pm rest of year) ■ Adm

Scotland's most famous poet was born in this tiny, two-room cottage in Alloway, which is now a museum dedicated to his life and work. It houses the world's finest collection of Burns memorabilia and original manuscripts, including "Auld Lang Syne". The surrounding heritage park includes the Burns Monument.

New Lanark on the River Clyde

3 New Lanark

MAP G4 ■ (01555) 661345 ■ www.newlanark.org ■ Apr–Oct: 10am–5pm; Nov–Mar: 11am–5pm ■ Adm

In 1820, at the height of the Industrial Revolution, factory owner Robert Owen recognized the need for safe and efficient working conditions, matched by good-quality housing for his workers. New Lanark was the result, a modern industrial town that also boasted an education system (including the world's first nursery school) and free healthcare. Now a UNESCO World Heritage Site, this living museum is still pioneering.

4 Traquair House

MAP G5 ■ Innerleithen ■ (01896) 830323 ■ www.traquair. co.uk ■ Apr–Sep: 11am–5pm; Oct: 11am–4pm; Nov: 11am–3pm Sat & Sun ■ Adm

Wonderfully atmospheric, Traquair dates back to 1107 and is Scotland's oldest inhabited house. The interior includes a hidden room leading to secret stairs along which Catholic priests could escape during persecutions. Bonnie Prince Charlie once stayed here.

5 Manderston House

MAP F6 ■ Duns ■ (01361) 883450 ■ www.manderston.co.uk ■ May–Sep: house 1:30–5pm Thu & Sun, gardens 11:30am–dusk ■ Adm

Set in 230,000 sq m (270,000 sq yards), this stunning Edwardian mansion was built to impress Scottish society. The most lavish feature of the interior is the silver staircase; there are also fine artworks and antiques.

Bass Rock
Dunbar
St Abb's Head
Cranshaws
Grantshouse 8
Manderston House 5
Berwick-upon-Tweed
Melrose Abbey
Mellerstain House 4
Holy Island
2 7 10
Dryburgh Abbey
Kirk
Jedburgh
Alnwick
Hawick
Kielder Water
North Tyne
Newcastle upon Tyne
Carlisle
Penrith

6 Linlithgow Palace

MAP F5 ■ Linlithgow ■ (01506) 842896 ■ Apr–Sep: 9:30am–5:30pm daily; Oct–Mar: 10am–4pm daily ■ Adm

Mary Queen of Scots

One of only four royal palaces in Scotland, Linlithgow was the birthplace of Mary Queen of Scots and provided a temporary safe haven for Bonnie Prince Charlie during the Jacobite Rebellion *(see p38)*. Solid and fortress-like on the banks of Linlithgow Loch, the palace still looks majestic in its semi-ruined state. This was the finest building of its day, and its master masons have left a wealth of carvings. Look around the Great Hall and chapel and marvel at the expertise of the craftsmen who laboured upon this wonderful building.

7 Rosslyn Chapel

MAP F5 ■ Rosslyn ■ (0131) 440 2159 ■ www.rosslyn-chapel.com ■ 9:30am–5pm Mon–Sat (until 6pm Apr–Sep), noon–4:45pm Sun ■ Adm

As extraordinary as it is mysterious. You'd be hard pushed to cram more carvings into such a small place. Built in 1446, it seems that every master mason had to do a turn here,

Intricate carvings in Rosslyn Chapel

such is the variety of styles and subjects. Most curious of all are the carvings of New World plants. They predate Columbus's transatlantic voyage of discovery by 100 years. The chapel has become extremely popular since featuring in the book and film *The Da Vinci Code*.

8 Melrose Abbey

MAP G5 ■ Melrose ■ (01896) 822562 ■ Apr–Sep: 9:30am–5.30pm daily; Oct–Mar: 10am–4pm daily ■ Adm

The tall lancet windows of this impressive ruin must have appeared miraculous to medieval worshippers. And today, it's hard to believe that such monuments could have been built as early as 1136. Over the centuries, the abbey succumbed to pillage and war damage, and now stands as a beleaguered but romantic spot for the ghost of Robert the Bruce, whose heart is believed to reside here.

Melrose Abbey

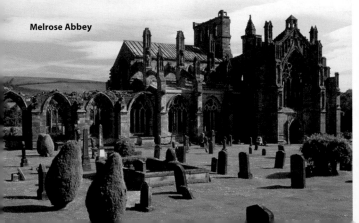

⑨ Mellerstain House

MAP G6 ■ Gordon ■ (01573)
410225 ■ www.mellerstain.com
■ Easter & May–Oct: 12:30–5pm
Fri–Mon ■ Adm

Scotland's most splendid Georgian
house (early 18th century) is another
creation by architect Robert Adam.
A vast edifice of perfect symmetry
on the outside contains rooms of
perfect proportions within. The
delicate plasterwork of the library,
resembling fine china, is considered
one of Adam's greatest accomplish-
ments. Exquisite details abound
throughout the interior, while
outside, grand terraced gardens
run down to an ornamental lake.

Mellerstain House

⑩ Dryburgh Abbey

MAP G6 ■ Nr St Boswells
■ (01835) 822381 ■ www.historic-
scotland.gov.uk ■ Apr–Sep:
9:30am–5:30pm daily; Oct–Mar:
10am–4pm daily ■ Adm

Located on a bend in the River
Tweed, these are the most beautiful
and evocative ruins in southern
Scotland. Founded in 1152, the abbey
was destroyed by the English in 1322,
1344 and again in 1385, but each
time it rose to magnificence once
more, until it was finally consumed
by fire in 1544. Despite having lain in
ruin for 500 years, it is remarkably
complete, and the quality of masonry
is unbelievable. See it when shadows
fall for the most spectacular views.

A TOUR OF THE BORDERS

▶ **MORNING**

Shop at the **Edinburgh Famers'
Market** or **Iain Mellis** (for both
see p79) the day before your trip
to make a gourmet picnic – as
simple or as lavish as you like.

The next morning, set off at 9am,
just after rush hour, and drive to
Rosslyn Chapel to see the extraordinary carvings. As wonderful
as they are, this stop won't take
long. So, before being tempted to
delve into the hamper, drive on to
Penicuik and take the A703 to
Peebles. It's worth having a break
for coffee in this pretty town.

Now take the lovely Tweedside
A72, then bear off onto the B7062
to reach **Traquair House** (see
p85). Explore this fascinating
building, which is still home to
the Maxwell-Stuart family, then
enjoy lunch at one of the picnic
tables in the extensive grounds.

AFTERNOON

Return to the A72, then continue
to visit either **Abbotsford House**
(see p88), the home of Sir Walter
Scott, or drive a bit further to the
romantic ruins of **Dryburgh
Abbey**, where the great writer is
buried. Both properties, which
close about 5pm, are a short
drive from **Scott's View**, from
where you can see the Eildon
Hills while you delve once more
into your picnic hamper for
afternoon tea.

Return to Edinburgh for your
evening meal or continue to
explore the Borders at your
leisure if you haven't had enough.

See map on pp84–5 ←

The Best of the Rest

Caerlaverock Castle

1 Caerlaverock Castle
MAP H5 ■ 13 km (8 miles) SE of Dumfries on the B725 ■ (01387) 770244 ■ www.historic-scotland.gov.uk ■ Adm
This triangular castle within a moat makes a stunning sight. It is remarkably complete, despite having been ruined for over 400 years.

2 Abbotsford House
MAP G5 ■ Nr Melrose ■ (01896) 752043 ■ www.scottsabbotsford.com ■ Mar & Nov: 10am–4pm daily; Apr–Oct: 10am–5pm daily ■ Adm
Home of the great novelist Sir Walter Scott, crammed with historical bric-a-brac. A short drive away on the B6356 is Scott's View.

3 Drumlanrig Castle
MAP G4 ■ Thornhill, Dumfries and Galloway ■ (01848) 331555 ■ www.drumlanrigcastle.co.uk ■ Castle: Jul, Aug, Easter and May holidays 11am–5pm; grounds: Apr–Sep 10am–5pm ■ Adm
This lavish 1676 castle of turrets and domes is home to the Duke of Buccleuch. It's filled with treasures.

4 Falkirk Wheel
MAP F4 ■ Falkirk ■ (08700) 500208 ■ www.thefalkirkwheel.co.uk ■ Visitor centre: 10am–5:30pm daily ■ Adm (for boat trips)
This engineering marvel is a "world's first"; revolving scoops connect two canal systems on different levels. Canal boats enter a giant "bucket", the wheel revolves and boats are moved. Visitors can take boat trips.

5 Kirkcudbright
MAP H4 ■ Dumfries and Galloway ■ www.kirkcudbright.co.uk
Pronounced "kirkoobree", this town and artists' colony has a ruined castle and was home to artist E A Hornel. This is a great place to buy quality, locally made arts and crafts.

6 Scottish Seabird Centre
MAP F5 ■ North Berwick ■ (01620) 890202 ■ www.seabird.org ■ Apr–Aug: 10am–6pm daily; closes earlier rest of year ■ Adm
Remote cameras relay live action from the Bass Rock's 100,000 gannets. Take time for a boat trip *(see p65)*.

7 Galloway Forest Park
MAP H4 ■ www.galloway forestpark.com
Area of superb loch, forest and hill scenery. Picnic at Bruce's Stone or have a day out on foot or on bikes.

8 St Abb's Head
MAP F6 ■ Visitor centre: (01890) 771443 ■ Apr–Oct: 10am–5pm daily
A national nature reserve on dramatic cliffs packed with birds. Don't miss the characterful town of St Abb's with its fishery museum.

9 Wigtown
MAP H4 ■ www.wigtown-booktown.co.uk
Pretty market town that has become a "book town", full of all sorts of literary specialities and events.

10 Floors Castle
MAP G6 ■ Kelso ■ (01573) 223333 ■ www.roxburghe.net/castle ■ Easter–Apr & Oct: 10:30am–3:30pm daily; May–Sep: 10:30am–5pm daily ■ Adm
Get a real taste of Downton Abbey at this magnificent property built in 1721 for the first Duke of Roxburghe and still the family home.

Places to Eat

PRICE CATEGORIES
For a three-course meal for one with half a bottle of wine (or equivalent meal), taxes and extra charges.

£ under 30   ££ £30–60   £££ over £60

1 Sorn Inn
MAP G4 ■ 25 Main St, Sorn, Ayrshire ■ (01290) 551305 ■ ££

Family-friendly country pub serving quality classics like steak pie, roast chicken and haddock and chips.

2 The Castle Restaurant
MAP H4 ■ 5 Castle St, Kirkcudbright ■ (01557) 330569 ■ ££

The French-influenced cuisine at The Castle is created using organic ingredients whenever possible.

3 Cobbles Inn
MAP G6 ■ 7 Bowmont St, Kelso ■ (01573) 223548 ■ ££

Popular town-centre gastropub offering bar lunches, fine dining in the evening, and craft beers from the nearby Tempest microbrewery.

4 Wheatsheaf at Swinton
MAP G6 ■ The Green, Swinton ■ (01890) 860257 ■ ££

Local lamb, fish and game are on the menu at this smart, country-style restaurant with a lovely setting overlooking the village green.

5 Peebles Hydro
MAP G5 ■ Innerleithen Rd, Peebles ■ (01721) 720602 ■ ££

The changing menu at this ornate restaurant features international cuisine and traditional dishes, with emphasis on seasonal, local food. The dress code is smart.

6 Wildings Restaurant
MAP G4 ■ Harbour Rd, Maidens, Ayrshire ■ (01655) 331401 ■ ££

An attractive restaurant with Isle of Arran views. The seasonal menu uses local ingredients. Book ahead.

7 Marmions
MAP G5 ■ Buccleuch St, Melrose ■ (01896) 822245 ■ Closed Sun ■ ££

Long-running French-style brasserie, popular with both locals and visitors. Snacks, an à la carte menu and wines for all tastes.

8 Tibbie Shiels Inn
MAP G5 ■ St. Mary's Loch, Selkirk ■ (01750) 42231 ■ £

This place offers an "olde worlde" pub atmosphere along with a bold menu, including four different vegetarian dishes daily.

9 Braidwoods
MAP G4 ■ Drumastle Mill Cottage, Dalry, Ayrshire ■ (01294) 833544 ■ ££

Four- to six-week waits are an indication of the quality on offer. Braidwoods fuses indigenous produce with a multicultural approach to a craft that takes in French and Italian influences.

10 Knockinaam Lodge
MAP H3 ■ Portpatrick ■ (01776) 810471 ■ £££

Traditional food with a modern touch in a sumptuous country house. Memorable seafood, such as a simple dish of pan-seared scallops. A five-course tasting menu offers the best of the kitchen.

Knockinaam Lodge

See map on pp84–5

TOP10 North and East of Edinburgh

A 2-hour drive from the centre of Edinburgh takes you either into the majestic Highland-like landscape of Perthshire, or through the rich farmland of Fife, with its coastal fringe of pretty seaside villages. This

Culross

area is Scotland arguably at its most diverse, with famous castles, abbeys, ships, bridges, wildlife reserves and golf courses all found within easy reach of each other by car. Golf is Scotland's greatest sporting tradition, and it is much in evidence here – especially in St Andrews, the sport's spiritual home. The many castles and palaces are testament to the enduring appeal of this pleasing and photogenic region.

AREA MAP OF THE NORTH AND EAST OF EDINBURGH

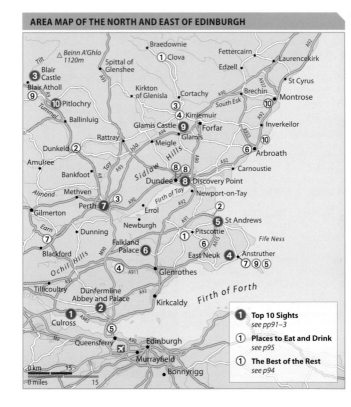

Braedownie
Beinn A'Ghlo 1120m
Spittal of Glenshee
1 Clova
Fettercairn
Laurencekirk
Edzell
3 Blair Castle
Blair Atholl
9
Kirkton of Glenisla
Cortachy
Brechin
St Cyrus
10 Pitlochry
3
South Esk
10 Montrose
Ballinluig
4 Kirriemuir
Glamis Castle
9 Forfar
Inverkeilor
10
Dunkeld **2**
Rattray
Meigle
Glamis
Arbroath **6**
Amulree
Bankfoot
Sidlaw Hills
Carnoustie
Methven
8 **8**
Dundee **8** Discovery Point
Perth **7**
Firth of Tay
Newport-on-Tay
Gilmerton
Errol
2
7
Dunning
Newburgh
St Andrews **5**
Falkland Palace **6**
1 Pitscottie
Fife Ness
Blackford
4
6
East Neuk **4** Anstruther
Glenrothes
7 **9** **5**
Ochil Hills
4
Tillicoultry
Dunfermline Abbey and Palace
Kirkcaldy
Firth of Forth
Culross **1**
2
5
Queensferry
Edinburgh
Murrayfield
Bonnyrigg
0 km   15
0 miles   15

1 Top 10 Sights
see pp91–3

1 Places to Eat and Drink
see p95

1 The Best of the Rest
see p94

1 Culross

MAP F5 ■ Palace: (0844) 493 2189 ■ www.nts.org.uk ■ Apr, May & Sep: noon–5pm Thu–Mon; Jun–Aug: noon–5pm daily; Oct: noon–4pm Thu–Mon; Garden: noon–4pm daily

Once a thriving village with mines, iron workings and trade links with the Low Countries, Culross fell into decline in the 18th and 19th centuries. Its restoration began in the 1930s, and now the town is a striking resurrection of its 16th- and 17th-century heyday.

2 Dunfermline Abbey and Palace

MAP F5 ■ Dunfermline ■ (01383) 724586 ■ www.dunfermlineabbey. co.uk ■ Apr–Oct: 10am–4:30pm Mon–Sat, 2:30–4:30pm Sun ■ Adm

Founded in the 11th century by Queen (later St) Margaret (see p13), the abbey's stunning feature is the 12th-century Romanesque nave. This was the burial place of Robert the Bruce – without his heart, which he requested be taken on a Crusade to the Holy Land. A skeleton with the heart chamber cut open was discovered in a grave here in 1818; the site is now marked by a plaque to honour the hero of the Battle of Bannockburn (see p38).

3 Blair Castle

MAP E4 ■ Blair Atholl ■ (01796) 481207 ■ www.blair-castle.co.uk ■ Apr–Oct: 9:30am–5:30pm ■ Adm

This striking castle is the ancestral seat of the Dukes of Atholl. Dating from 1269, it has been extended over

Blair Castle and the hills of Perthshire

the centuries and boasts crenellations, turrets and a grand ballroom. Queen Victoria was so impressed when she stayed that she gave the then Duke permission to raise a private army. You may see one of his Atholl Highlanders playing the bagpipes in summer.

4 East Neuk

MAP F5–6

Neuk is a Scots word for "corner", and the East Neuk refers to a small bend in the coastline along which is found a remarkable chain of picturesque fishing villages. They run from Earlsferry to Crail, and every one is a gem. Elie and Crail are probably the most quaint and are favoured haunts of artists. Pittenweem's beautiful harbour is still a working port, and Anstruther, a haven for yachts, has a bustling seafront. The Scottish Fisheries Museum (see p94) is excellent and worth a stop.

Picturesque coastal village of East Neuk

The ruins of St Andrews Cathedral

5 St Andrews

MAP F5 ■ Cathedral & Castle Apr–Sep: 9:30am–5:30pm daily; Oct–Mar: 10am–4pm daily ■ Adm

The "home of golf" *(see p58)* has the oldest university in Scotland, and red-robed students add a colourful, carefree atmosphere to this pretty town. St Andrews was once the ecclesiastical capital of the country and its cathedral is still a proud ruin, with a wealth of sculpture. Its castle has unrivalled examples of siege tunnels and a curious "bottle dungeon". There's also a long beach for fine walks, and plenty of hip cafés and bistros.

HOME OF GOLF

The coastal links courses around St Andrews are recognized as the birthplace of golf – the earliest record of the game being played here dates to 1457. Golfing heritage continues in the city to this day, and St Andrew's Royal and Ancient Golf Club remains the ruling arbiter of the game.

6 Falkland Palace

MAP F5 ■ Falkland ■ (0844) 493 2186 ■ www.nts.org.uk ■ Mar–Oct: 11am–5pm Mon–Sat, noon–5pm Sun ■ Adm

A wonderful sense of history pervades this palace, the home of Mary Queen of Scots and the Stuart kings from 1541. Restored royal bedchambers and fine 17th-century tapestries are on display, but most intriguing of all is the oldest real tennis court still in use in Britain, built in 1539. Unlike

Falkland Palace crest

the modern game, real tennis was played indoors and shares some similarities with squash.

7 Perth and Scone Palace

MAP E5 ■ Palace: (01738) 552300; www.scone-palace.co.uk ; May–Sep: 9:30am–5:30pm (to 4pm Apr & Oct); Nov–Mar: grounds only 10am–4pm Fri–Sun; Adm (grounds free)

The "Fair City", as Perth is known, is attractively situated on the tree-lined River Tay. Its streets are a delight of small shops for browsing. Just north of the city, off the A93, is Scone Palace. The grounds contain the Moot Hill, where Scottish kings were crowned on the famous Stone of Destiny, now in Edinburgh Castle.

8 Discovery Point
MAP E5 ■ Dundee ■ (01382) 309060 ■ www.rrsdiscovery.com ■ Apr–Oct: 10am–6pm daily (from 11am Sun); Nov–Mar: 10am–5pm daily (from 11am Sun) ■ Adm

The full chill and hazards of Antarctic exploration grip you in this superb hi-tech exhibition. Focusing on the heroic and tragic expeditions of Shackleton and Scott, this display uses original film footage as well as stunning modern images and interactive computer screens. The highlight is a tour of the Dundee-built boat RSS *Discovery*, the one that carried Scott and his companions on their ill-fated expedition. (While in Dundee check out the Contemporary Arts Centre on Nethergate for great exhibitions and its fine bistro-café.)

9 Glamis Castle
A royal residence since 1372, this is a magical castle. Towers and turrets, treasures and a link with Shakespeare's *Macbeth* – could you ask for more in a castle? *(See p42.)*

Glamis Castle

10 Pitlochry
MAP E4/5 ■ www.pitlochry.org. uk ■ Theatre: (01796) 484626 ■ Information Centre: 22 Atholl Rd; (01796) 472215; 9:30am–4:30pm Mon–Sat, 11am–3pm Sun

This tartan-and-tweed town has a long history of serving visitors. Its proximity to Perthshire's beauty spots and sporting estates was the original draw, but now it boasts a fine theatre and a fish ladder, where salmon leap up a series of pools to reach spawning grounds. A perfect introduction to the joys of Scotland.

AN EAST COAST DRIVE

▶ MORNING

Leave Edinburgh around 9am and make for **South Queensferry** to photograph the iconic **Forth Bridges** *(see p94)*. There's an information centre where you can find out about the history of the bridges, and about the Queensferry Crossing.

Cross the road bridge and take the M90 to **Perth**. Stroll around the town, have a coffee, then follow the A93 to **Scone Palace** to see where Scottish kings such as Macbeth and Robert the Bruce were crowned. If you're hungry, have lunch here; they source ingredients from the palace kitchen garden.

Now it's about an hour's drive, via the A90 to **Dundee** where you can stop at **Discovery Point** and shiver at the exploits of the Antarctic explorers. Otherwise cross the **Tay Bridge**, then join the A919 to reach **St Andrews**, home to Scotland's oldest university and most famous golf course. There are plenty of places to eat.

AFTERNOON

You could easily spend the rest of the day strolling around St Andrews' quaint streets, but if you continue along the coast you'll come to the East Neuk fishing villages of **Crail** and **Pittenweem** *(see p91)* – not forgetting lovely **Anstruther**, where you'll find the **Scottish Fisheries Museum** *(see p94)*. Relax, soak up the scenery and enjoy a meal in one of the excellent fish restaurants.

See map on p90 ←

The Best of the Rest

① Hill of Tarvit Mansion
MAP F5 ▪ Cupar ▪ (01334) 653127 ▪ House Apr–Oct: 1–5pm Wed–Sun (daily from late Jun–Aug); grounds 9am–dusk daily ▪ www.nts.org.uk ▪ Adm

This 17th-century mansion with extensive grounds was remodelled in 1906 for a wealthy industrialist.

② Dunkeld
MAP E5

A village of great charm and character, with the noble ruins of its 14th-century cathedral and gorgeous riverside walks.

③ Kirriemuir and the Angus Glens
MAP E5

J M Barrie, creator of Peter Pan, was born in Kirriemuir; his birthplace is now a museum. Nearby are the wild and beautiful Angus Glens, great for scenic hikes.

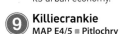

Peter Pan statue, Kirriemuir

④ Loch Leven
MAP F5 ▪ Adm

Mary, Queen of Scots, was imprisoned in the now ruined castle here. The loch provides a haven for birds – including ospreys.

⑤ Forth Bridges
MAP F5

The iconic cantilever rail bridge and tall, suspension road bridge are best seen lit up at night.

⑥ Arbroath Abbey
MAP E6 ▪ Apr–Sep: 9:30am–5:30pm daily; Oct–Mar: 10am–4pm daily ▪ Adm

The abbey makes for impressive ruins, but it's most famous for the "Declaration of Arbroath", Scotland's eloquent charter for independence, a copy of which is on show.

⑦ Scottish Fisheries Museum
MAP F5 ▪ Anstruther ▪ (01333) 310628 ▪ www.scotfishmuseum.org ▪ Adm

It's hard to believe just how fascinating boats, nets and fish can be. First-class overview of the history of the fish supper.

⑧ Verdant Works
MAP E5 ▪ Dundee ▪ (01382) 309060 ▪ www.verdantworks.com ▪ Adm

Voted "European Industrial Museum of the Year", this is an invigorating presentation of the jute industry, the material upon which Dundee founded its urban economy.

⑨ Killiecrankie
MAP E4/5 ▪ Pitlochry

The combined attractions of a famous battle site and an idyllic river gorge. Admire the famous Soldier's Leap, but don't try it! Queen Victoria loved this spot (and she was famously hard to please).

⑩ Montrose Basin Wildlife Centre
MAP E6 ▪ (01674) 676336 ▪ www.montrosebasin.org.uk ▪ Mar–Oct: 10:30am–5pm daily; Nov–Feb: 10:30am–4pm Fri–Sun ▪ Adm

Montrose is a tidal basin mecca for seafowl and waders. In autumn, 35,000 pink-footed geese stop here during their migration.

Forth Rail Bridge from Queensferry Harbour

Places to Eat and Drink

PRICE CATEGORIES

For a three-course meal for one with half a bottle of wine (or equivalent meal), taxes and extra charges.

£ under £30   ££ £30–60   £££ over £60

1 Glen Clova Hotel
MAP E5 ■ Glen Clova, nr Kirriemuir ■ (01575) 550350 ■ ££

Situated at the end of a lovely glen is this hotel and restaurant. A simple all-day menu provides such staples as haddock, venison and home-made pies, while slightly more elaborate dishes are served for dinner.

2 Old Course Hotel
MAP F5 ■ St Andrews ■ (01334) 474371 ■ ££

For lovers of traditional fine dining, the hotel's Road Hole Restaurant offers French-influenced cuisine, whereas the menu at Sands Grill is more cosmopolitan, journeying from North Africa to Italy.

3 63 Tay Street
MAP E5 ■ 63 Tay St, Perth ■ (01738) 441451 ■ Closed for dinner Sun & Mon ■ ££

This restaurant is the talk of the town, thanks to chef Graeme Pallister. An extensive wine list complements a thrilling menu, which makes full use of Perthshire's prime natural larder.

4 Café 88°
MAP E5 ■ 17 High St, Kirriemuir ■ (01575) 570888 ■ £

Deli and café with delicious, home-made light lunches. There are scattered newspapers and the best coffee and cakes for miles.

5 The Cellar
MAP F5 ■ Anstruther, Fife ■ (01333) 310378 ■ ££

A seafood heaven off a courtyard behind the Fisheries Museum. One meat dish, plus some of the best fish in Scotland.

The Peat Inn

6 The Peat Inn
MAP F5 ■ Cupar ■ (01334) 840206 ■ ££

Exceptional food and range of wine at the fairest prices. This restaurant is an enduring favourite (see p68).

7 Andrew Fairlie
MAP F4 ■ Gleneagles Hotel ■ (01764) 694267 ■ Closed Sun ■ £££

French cuisine of high calibre served amid dreamy 1920s decor (see p68).

8 Jute Café Bar
MAP E5 ■ Dundee Contemporary Arts Centre, 152 Nethergate, Dundee ■ (01382) 909246 ■ ££

The cavernous interior at the Jute Café Bar is ultrahip. There is a range of beers available and the menu offers both imaginative dishes and very reasonable prices.

9 Ship Inn
MAP F5 ■ Elie, nr Anstruther ■ (01333) 330246 ■ ££

Plain no-nonsense food served in a converted boathouse overlooking the harbour of this much-photographed village. Bar below, bistro above.

10 The But 'n' Ben
MAP E6 ■ Auchmithie, nr Abroath ■ (01241) 877223 ■ ££

Within the white walls of this old fisherman's cottage, seafood is the speciality, naturally enough (especially Arbroath Smokies, see p69). You'll also find good venison and local produce here.

See map on p90

TOP 10 Glasgow

Stained-glass window, Glasgow Cathedral

Edinburgh may be the pretty sister, but Glasgow arguably has the more dynamic character, as exemplified by the outgoing and friendly Glaswegians. From the highs and lows of its storied past, the city of Glasgow has endured. Today it has reinvented itself as something of an epicentre of culture, cuisine, shopping and entertainment. Magnificent buildings are scattered right across the city, along with Michelin-starred restaurants, while the patronage of wealthy collectors has ensured the exceptional quality of Glasgow's many museums, art galleries and gardens.

AREA MAP OF GLASGOW

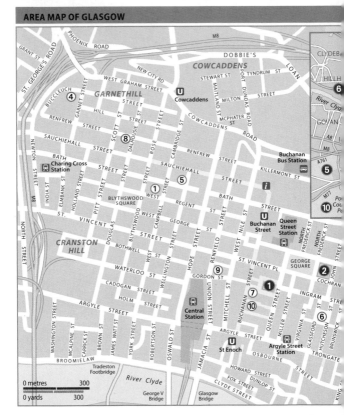

Gallery of Modern Art

MAP T4 ■ Royal Exchange Square ■ (0141) 287 3050 ■ 10am–5pm daily (from 11am Fri–Sun; to 8pm Thu)

Glasgow's Gallery of Modern Art, or, more correctly, "of Astonishment", includes some works that immediately grab your attention, others that are deviously clever and a few that are outrageously funny. Exhibits change frequently, but the ethos remains essentially the same. Three main galleries feature painting, sculpture and modern photography in addition to permanent works by Scottish artists such as Peter Howson, Toby Paterson and John Byrne. In the basement is a sofa-adorned library, with a café and free Internet access.

City Chambers

City Chambers

MAP U4 ■ George Square ■ (0141) 287 4018 ■ www.glasgow.gov.uk ■ By official tour only: 10:30am & 2:30pm Mon–Fri

"Palace" would be a more appropriate term, for this is the finest seat of any council in Britain. Modelled on Classical Italian architecture, the building was designed by William Young and completed in 1888. The exterior is dramatic enough, but the interior is an exercise in the excesses of lavish decor. Aberdeen granite, Carrara marble, mahogany, gold leaf, frescoes, mosaics, pillars and balustrades are combined to astonishing effect. The Banqueting Hall – with its murals, chandeliers and ornately patterned ceiling and carpet – cannot fail to impress even the most jaded of visitors.

Glasgow Cathedral and Necropolis

MAP V3 ■ Cathedral Square ■ (0141) 552 6891 ■ 9:30am–5:30pm Mon–Sat, 1–5pm Sun (to 4pm Oct–Mar)

Immense and ancient, this cathedral was ranked by Pope Nicholas V in 1451 as equal in merit to Rome as a place of pilgrimage. Dedicated in 1136 and completed almost a century later, it has been in continuous use since then and can boast original roof timbers. The choir screen is unique in Scotland, and the post-war stained-glass windows are exceptional. On a hill to the east looms the Necropolis, an extravagance of tombstones that is crowned by a monument to John Knox (see p14).

Top 10 Sights
see pp97–9

Places to Eat and Drink
see p101

The Best of the Rest
see p100

4 Kelvingrove Art Gallery and Museum

The most-visited collection in Scotland underwent a major refurbishment that doubled the museum's capacity, and provided the chance to display previously unseen works. Best of the bunch in Glasgow *(see pp20–21)*.

Stained glass, House for an Art Lover

5 House for an Art Lover

MAP U2 ■ Bellahouston Park, Dumbreck Rd ■ (0141) 353 4770 ■ www.houseforanartlover.co.uk ■ 10am–4pm Mon–Thu but times vary, so call ahead ■ Adm

In 1901 Glasgow's tour-de-force architect, Charles Rennie Mackintosh, and his artist wife, Margaret Macdonald, entered a magazine competition to design a "House for an Art Lover". It was to be "a grand house, thoroughly modern, fresh and innovative". Their exquisite vision remained just a design until 1989, when, authentic to the smallest detail, the building and its contents were created. The café and shop are superb.

6 Riverside Museum

MAP U2 ■ 1 Bunhouse Rd ■ (0141) 287 2720 ■ www.glasgow museums.com ■ 10am–5pm daily (from 11am Fri & Sun)

Bicycles, cars, lorries, buses, trains, fire engines ... hundreds and hundreds of everything on wheels in acres of gleaming metalwork. You can walk through or climb into the larger vehicles, or sit in an original Glasgow tram. Upstairs are 250 model ships illustrating the story of Clyde shipbuilding. Watch out for the penny on the cobbles of the re-created 1938 shopping street – but don't try to pick it up, or you could be there all day.

7 People's Palace

MAP V3 ■ Glasgow Green ■ (0141) 276 0788 ■ www.glasgow museums.com ■ 10am–5pm Tue–Sun (from 11am Fri & Sun)

Typically Glaswegian, this is a museum of ordinary life. Nothing fancy or outstandingly old, but a fascinating insight into how the average family lived, worked and played in the not-so-distant past. The tranquil Winter Gardens are connected to the museum.

8 Science Centre

Myriad puzzles, experiments and demonstrations to entertain and inform. There's also an IMAX screen and a revolving tower – a sensational place *(see p65)*.

Science Centre

Kibble Palace, Botanic Gardens

9 Botanic Gardens

MAP U2 ■ 730 Great Western Rd, Glasgow ■ (0141) 276 1614 ■ Gardens: 7am–dusk daily; Glasshouses: 10am–6pm daily (4:15pm winter)

The highlights are the glasshouses famous for their tropicana (see p55).

10 Burrell Collection and Pollok Park

MAP U3 ■ Pollokshaws Rd ■ (0141) 616 6410 ■ www.nts.org.uk ■ House: 10am–5pm ■ Adm

Sir William Burrell's (1861–1958) superb collection, housed in a purpose-designed building in Pollok Country Park, has long been one of Glasgow's finest attractions. The Burrell Collection will be closed for major works from 2016, but nearby Pollok House is worth a visit. It gives a fascinating insight into Edwardian life and boasts Spanish paintings by Murillo, El Greco and Goya. There's a cafe in the original kitchen, and plenty of lovely walks in the surrounding wooded parkland.

ST MUNGO

A priest called St Mungo laid the foundations of Glasgow when he set up a monastery here in the 6th century. A settlement grew up around the monastery and prospered long after the demise of that early religious community. St Mungo's body lies beneath the cathedral, and his name has been given to a museum of religious art (see p100).

A FULL DAY IN GLASGOW

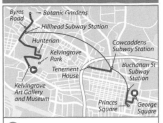

▶ MORNING

Take the subway to Kelvinhall station (or walk from the city centre) to visit **Kelvingrove Art Gallery and Museum**. Allow a couple of hours to explore and don't miss the Dutch Old Masters and French Impressionists.

Now it's easiest to walk to the **Hunterian** (see p100), on the other side of **Kelvingrove Park**, to take a tour of the stunning House for an Art Lover, a reassemblage of the interiors of Charles Rennie Mackintosh's home. Tours start at 10am (11am on Sunday). Lunch at one of the many cafés on the nearby **Byres Road** or walk on to reach the **Botanic Gardens**, where you can picnic in the grounds or enjoy a meal in their tearoom. Stroll through the gardens and admire the orchids in the enormous, tropical Kibble Palace glasshouse.

AFTERNOON

Take the subway to **Cowcaddens** station, from where it's a short walk to the **Tenement House** (see p100). This intriguing, gas-lit property is laid out much as it was when it was home to Agnes Toward in the early 20th century; it's a real slice of old Glasgow life.

Hop back on the subway to **Buchanan Street** station, where you can choose to walk down to elegant **Princes Square** (see p100) to browse the shops, or make your way across **George Square** in time for the 2:30pm tour of the **City Chambers** (see p97). Have dinner in one of the city's many restaurants (see p101).

See map on pp96–7 ⬅

The Best of the Rest

1 St Mungo Museum of Religious Art
MAP V3 ■ 2 Castle St
■ (0141) 276 1625

Excellent overview of the world's religions through their art. The museum is illuminated by beautiful stained-glass windows.

2 Waverley Excursions
MAP S4 ■ Anderston Quay
■ (0845) 130 4647 ■ www.waverley excursions.co.uk ■ Jun–Aug

Travel back in time and experience the Firth of Clyde on the world's last seagoing paddle steamer.

3 Hunterian Art Gallery
MAP U2 ■ 82 Hillhead St, nr Kelvingrove Park ■ (0141) 330 4221 ■ www.gla.ac.uk/hunterian ■ 10am–5pm Tue–Sat, 11am–4pm Sun

This gallery is best known for its collection of Rembrandts, its works by 19th-century American artist Whistler and the Mackintosh House.

4 Tenement House
MAP S2 ■ 145 Buccleuch St
■ (0844) 493 2197 ■ Mar–Oct: 1–5pm daily ■ Adm

Tenements were standard Glasgow flats and Agnes Toward lived an ordinary life in this one, now a museum, for over 50 years.

5 Scotland Street School Museum
MAP V3 ■ 225 Scotland St ■ (0141) 287 0500 ■ 10am–5pm Tue–Thu & Sat, 11am–5pm Fri & Sun

Re-created Victorian, World War II and 1950s classrooms. Great fun.

6 Merchant City
MAP U4

East of George Square is this grid-plan of streets where the "Tobacco Lords" built their warehouses and mansions. The area is now full of designer shops and restaurants.

7 Provand's Lordship
MAP V2 ■ 3 Castle St ■ (0141) 276 1625 ■ 10am–5pm Tue–Thu & Sat, 11am–5pm Fri & Sun

Built in 1471, this is the oldest house in Glasgow, with a fine furniture collection and cloistered herb garden.

8 Glasgow School of Art
MAP S3 ■ 167 Renfrew St
■ (0141) 353 4526 ■ www.gsa.ac.uk ■ Visitor Centre: 10am–4:30pm daily; Daily tours offered, booking advised ■ Adm

A working college, this is architect and designer Charles Rennie Mackintosh's most famous building.

9 Citizens Theatre
MAP V3 ■ 119 Gorbals St
■ (0141) 429 0022 ■ www.citz.co.uk

An internationally famous venue; two modern studios complement the old Victorian auditorium.

10 Princes Square
MAP T4 ■ 48 Buchanan St
■ (0141) 221 0324

Luxurious shopping centre in a renovated square of 1841 – the genteel atmosphere found here is heightened by the occasional appearance of a piano player.

Princes Square shopping centre

Places to Eat and Drink

PRICE CATEGORIES

For a three-course meal for one with half a bottle of wine (or equivalent meal), taxes and extra charges.

£ under £30   ££ £30–60   £££ over £60

1 Brian Maule at Chardon D'Or

MAP T3 ▪ 176 West Regent St ▪ (0141) 248 3801 ▪ ££

A true fine-dining experience that should not be missed. The chef, Brian Maule, combines the greatness of classic French cuisine with modern dishes that use top-quality Scottish produce.

2 Ubiquitous Chip

MAP U2 ▪ 12 Ashton Lane, off Byres Rd, Hillhead ▪ (0141) 334 5007 ▪ ££

Operating on this cobbled West End road since 1971, and always a champion of Scottish produce, the Ubiquitous Chip restaurant is Glasgow at its most endearing.

3 Stravaigin

MAP U/V2 ▪ 28 Gibson St, Hillhead ▪ (0141) 334 2665 ▪ ££

Where the nation's fish, beef, lamb and game are mixed with the world's sauces, herbs and spices. Eclectic mix of flavours, but Stravaigin's judicious touch wins the day.

4 Firebird

MAP U3 ▪ 1321 Argyle St, nr Riverside Museum ▪ (0141) 334 0594 ▪ ££

Firebird is a popular hangout for easy drinks and great pizzas – it's simple and consistently good.

5 Fratelli Sarti

MAP T3 ▪ 121 Bath St & 133 Wellington St & 42 Renfield St ▪ (0141) 572 7000 ▪ ££

Lively Italian displaying a love of food in a living, breathing, everyday sense. Restaurant on Bath Street, with a café and deli around the corner.

6 Chinaski's

MAP W3 ▪ 239 North St ▪ (0141) 221 0061 ▪ £

The soundtrack here is one of the best in Glasgow, combining blues, soul and reggae. There is a heated deck and the food is enticing.

City Merchant

7 City Merchant

MAP U4 ▪ 97–99 Candleriggs ▪ (0141) 553 1577 ▪ ££

Looking like it's been around for aeons (though only in fact since the late 1980s), City Merchant is a Gallic-Scottish delight. Alongside some meaty mains, fish is the star.

8 Rogano

MAP T4 ▪ 11 Exchange Place, off Exchange Square ▪ (0141) 248 4055 ▪ ££

A wonderful place to imbibe splendid cocktails in Art Deco surrounds. Pricey in the restaurant but fresh seafood is a bargain in the brasserie.

9 The Horse Shoe Bar

MAP T4 ▪ 17 Drury St ▪ (0141) 248 6368 ▪ £

Few pubs deserve to be considered a Glasgow institution more than this gem of a place. Friendly and cheap, it is a cracking pub in which to soak up the city's ambience.

10 Mother India

MAP V2 ▪ 28 Westminster Terrace, Sauchiehall St ▪ (0141) 221 1663 ▪ ££

A must-visit destination for gourmands of all stripes. You'll find exquisite modern Indian food here.

See map on pp96–7

TOP 10 North and West of Glasgow

This bucolic region became the focus of Scotland's first tourist industry in early Victorian times and, with Loch Lomond and the Trossachs National Park at its splendid centre, that allure remains as strong today. In the west are the rocky peaks of the Isle of Arran and a seaboard of fjord-like lochs, where a mild climate supports some grand gardens. In the east stands Stirling – a key city in the country's warring past – its mighty clifftop castle overlooking lush farmland. Here, William Wallace and Robert the Bruce fought for independence, a battle eventually won within sight of the castle on the field of Bannockburn.

Wallace Monument

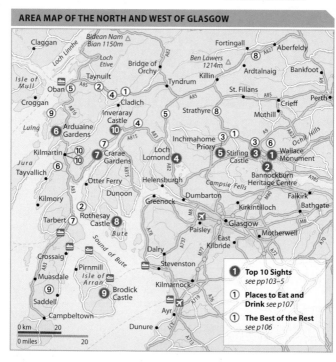

AREA MAP OF THE NORTH AND WEST OF GLASGOW

1	**Top 10 Sights** see pp103–5
1	**Places to Eat and Drink** see p107
1	**The Best of the Rest** see p106

1 Wallace Monument

MAP F4 ■ Apr–Jun, Sep & Oct: 10am–5pm daily; Jul & Aug: 10am–6pm daily; Nov–Mar: 10:30am–4pm daily ■ Adm

Erected in 1869, this 75-m (250-ft) tower commemorates William Wallace and his valiant fight for Scotland's independence. The climb to the top takes you past Wallace's two-handed broadsword, but most electrifying of all is the "talking head", which presents Wallace's defence before his brutal execution in 1305. There are splendid 360° views from the top.

Trossachs National Park

2 Bannockburn Heritage Centre

MAP F4 ■ Site open all year; Heritage Centre: Mar & Oct: 10am–5:30pm daily; Nov–Feb: 10am–5pm daily ■ Adm

The site of the decisive battle in 1314 (see p38) is marked by a visitor centre and an arresting equestrian statue of Robert the Bruce. At the centre, kids can try on helmets and chain mail, and view Bruce's cave to watch the fabled spider who inspired him to renew his fight.

Robert the Bruce, Bannockburn

3 Stirling Castle

MAP F4 ■ (01786) 450000 ■ Apr–Sep: 9:30am–6pm daily; Oct–Mar: 9:30am–5pm daily ■ Adm

Stirling Castle is a commanding rock-top affair, concealing architecture of an exceptional quality, most notably the restored Great Hall and the Royal Palace.

4 Loch Lomond and the Trossachs National Park

MAP F4 ■ www.lochlomond-trossachs.org

The broad, friendly mountains and poetic scenery of Scotland's first national park are ideal for the casual walker and watersports lover. Luss is the prettiest village in the area. It hosts a popular Highland Games (see p41) in June and has good tea shops. Cruises run from here, and from Balloch, Tarbet and Balmaha.

5 Inchmahome Priory

MAP F4 ■ (01877) 385294 ■ www.historic-scotland.gov.uk ■ Apr–Oct: 10am–4:15pm (Oct 3:15pm) daily ■ Adm

The Lake of Menteith is Scotland's only lake (as opposed to loch), and famed for the graceful ruined priory on the island of Inchmahome. It's in this beautiful spot that the infant Mary Queen of Scots was looked after by Augustinian monks before she was spirited away to France.

Stirling Castle

6 Arduaine Gardens
A dazzling assembly of rhododendrons, azaleas, magnolias and hosts of exotic species from the Pacific Islands to the Himalayas. Arduaine is beautifully situated on a promontory between sea lochs, and glories in the warm winds from the Gulf Stream *(see p55)*.

7 Crarae Gardens
You don't have to be a rhododendron specialist to be bowled over by this beautifully manicured orchestration of colour. An outstanding and rare collection, which is at its best in spring *(see p55)*.

8 Rothesay Castle, Bute
MAP F3 ■ (01700) 502691
■ Apr–Sep: 9:30am–5:30pm daily; Oct–Mar: 10am–4pm Mon–Wed, Sat & Sun ■ Adm

By virtue of its age, design and deep-water moat (one of only two remaining in Scotland), this is a remarkable medieval castle. Built

Rothesay Castle, Bute

around 1098 in the days of Norse occupation, it was restyled in the 13th century and fitted with high curtain walls and drum towers. Its circular courtyard is a curious feature and unique in Scotland. Bute itself is a mere 35-minute crossing from Wemyss Bay – north of Largs on the A78 – to Rothesay Bay; an even shorter crossing is from Colintraive to Rhubodach, on the north coast of the island.

THE WONDERFUL WORLD OF CRARAE GARDENS

Lady Grace Campbell laid out the gardens (**below**) in the 1920s, making exciting use of plant specimens that her nephew Reginald Farrer brought back from his travels to Tibet and the Himalayas. On the higher ground is the forest-garden, a feature that is found nowhere else in Britain, where more than 100 tree species grow under forest conditions on their own plots. Crarae is considered of international importance and is a member of "Glorious Gardens of Argyll and Bute" (www.gardens-of-argyll.co.uk).

---

9 Brodick Castle, Arran
MAP G3 ■ (0844) 493 2152
■ www.nts.org.uk ■ Castle: Apr–Oct: 11am–4pm daily (until 3pm Apr & Oct); Tearoom: 10am–4pm daily; Park: 9:30am–sunset daily ■ Adm

Originally a Viking keep before the Dukes of Hamilton claimed it, this 13th-century fortified tower was extended by Oliver Cromwell and then transformed into a stately home in Victorian times. The last Hamilton moved out only in 1957. A solid red sandstone building with fanciful trimmings, it contains a noted collection of silver, porcelain and paintings. The gardens are beautifully maintained (try to catch the rhododendrons in spring bloom), as are the woodland trails. The main ferry to Arran (just under an hour) is from Ardrossan, on the mainland coast, just north of Irvine.

10 Inveraray Castle
MAP F3 ▪ (01499) 302203
▪ www.inveraray-castle.com ▪ Apr–
Oct: 10am–5:45pm daily ▪ Adm

Despite the ravages of fire, Clan Campbell's family seat is a splendid pseudo-Gothic palace with pointed towers. It was built for the Duke of Argyll in 1745. The interiors were designed by Robert Mylne and contain Regency furniture and priceless works of art. The Armoury Hall was stocked to fight the Jacobites. There's a hilltop folly in the grounds. The castle hosts the popular Connect music festival in late August, when it is temporarily closed to visitors.

Armoury Hall, Inveraray Castle

A DAY IN THE TROSSACHS

▶ MORNING

Reserve your morning cruise on the SS *Sir Walter Scott* (call (01877) 87315 in advance).

Leaving **Glasgow** by 8:15am, drive north on the A81 to **Strathblane** and **Aberfoyle**. You are now in the scenic and famous **Trossachs** *(see p103)*. Park at the **Trossachs Pier** for your 10:30am cruise on **Loch Katrine**, a gorgeous secluded loch.

Arriving back at 12:30pm, a short drive takes you to Kilmahog (great walks, but the Woollen Mill is pretty touristy); pass it by unless you're overly curious about knitwear. Head on to **Callander**, where you can stop for lunch at one of several restaurants, or buy delicious pies at the **Scotch Oven**, a superb baker, and picnic by the river.

AFTERNOON

Carry on to **Doune**, **Dunblane** and **Bridge of Allan**. There are many temptations en route, including a castle *(see p106)*, a safari park and a motor museum.

If not, aim to be at the **Wallace Monument** *(see p103)* before 4pm. The history here is accompanied by panoramic views of the area, including the craggy heights of **Stirling Castle** *(see p103)*.

Finally, wend your way up into moorland for dinner at the **Sheriffmuir Inn** *(see p107)*. Head back to Glasgow or further east to Edinburgh or St Andrews (each about an hour's drive).

See map on p102 ←

The Best of the Rest

Kilchurn Castle

1 Kilchurn Castle
MAP E3 ■ Open access

Hauntingly atmospheric ruins of a Campbell castle, built in 1440 on an island to the northeast of Loch Awe. The picturesque ruins are visible from many vantage points.

2 Bonawe Historic Iron Furnace
MAP E3 ■ Taynuilt ■ (01866) 822432 ■ www.historic-scotland.gov.uk ■ Apr–Sep: 9:30am–5:30pm daily ■ Adm

The best-preserved charcoal-fuelled ironworks in Britain. Learn how iron was made here in 1753 in this lovely setting by Loch Etive.

3 Doune Castle
MAP F4 ■ (01786) 841742 ■ Apr–Sep: 9:30am–5:30pm daily; Oct–Mar: 10am–4pm daily ■ Adm

This 14th-century castle has a magical air about it. Perhaps most enchanting is the Lord's Hall, with its musicians' gallery and double fireplace.

4 Cruachan Hollow Mountain Power Station
MAP E3 ■ Nr Lochawe ■ (01866) 822618 ■ www.visitcruachan.co.uk ■ Apr–Oct: 9:30am–4:45pm daily; Nov, Dec, Feb & Mar: 10am–3:45pm Mon–Fri ■ Adm

Tunnels and underground caverns make this massive hydroelectric plant seem like a science-fiction set.

5 Oban
MAP E3 ■ Visitor Info: (01631) 563122

Busy harbour town best viewed from McCaig's Folly. Many local attractions and ferries to Mull, Coll, Colonsay, Tiree and the Western Isles.

6 Crinan Canal
MAP F3

Take a stroll along this scenic 16-km (9-mile) canal, completed in 1801 and now used by yachts and fishing boats. The best places to see them are at Ardrishaig, Cairnbaan or Crinan.

7 Auchindrain Township
MAP F3 ■ Nr Inveraray ■ (01499) 500235 ■ www.auchindrain.org.uk ■ Apr–Oct: 10am–5pm daily ■ Adm

A novel outdoor museum of restored thatched cottages and outbuildings, Auchindrain displays the past styles of West Highland life.

8 Scottish Crannog Centre
MAP E4 ■ Kenmore ■ (01887) 830583 ■ www.crannog.co.uk ■ Apr–Oct: 10am–5:30pm daily ■ Adm

The little-known and ancient art of building crannogs (defensive homesteads built on stilts in lochs) has been rediscovered here at Loch Tay.

9 Kintyre
MAP G3 ■ Tourist Info: (01586) 552056

Paul McCartney sang about this glorious peninsula, which has miles of beaches, a top golf course (Machrihanish) and the ethereal cave crucifixion painting on Davaar Island.

10 Kilmartin Glen
MAP F3

Inhabited for 5,000 years, Kilmartin Glen has a phenomenal concentration of archaeological remains: standing stones, temples and burial cairns. Pause at Kilmartin Church for the best collection of early Christian crosses.

Places to Eat and Drink

PRICE CATEGORIES
For a three-course meal for one with half
a bottle of wine (or equivalent meal),
taxes and extra charges.

£ under £30   ££ £30–60   £££ over £60

1 The Roman Camp
MAP F4 ▪ Callander
▪ (01877) 330003 ▪ £££
Voluptuous curtains, deep sofas and
blazing fires make this country hotel
a delight, and the restaurant excels.
Their guinea fowl breast with truffle
noodles is a winner.

2 Marina Restaurant
MAP F3 ▪ Portavadie, Loch
Fyne ▪ (01700) 811075 ▪ ££
Fresh seafood and Loch Fyne
oysters are served in this lovely
restaurant that boasts splendid
views of the Kintyre and distant
Arran Hills.

3 Lake Of Menteith
MAP F4 ▪ Port of Menteith
▪ (01877) 385258 ▪ ££
Smart lakeside restaurant situated
in a lovely conservatory. The menu
serves well-executed Scottish fare.

Loch Fyne Oyster Bar

4 Loch Fyne Oyster Bar
MAP F3 ▪ Cairndow, nr
Inveraray ▪ (01499) 600482 ▪ ££
Long established in this converted
stone cattle byre, the oyster bar
offers two vegetarian dishes daily
and an ocean of the freshest
seafood. Bring a hearty appetite and
have a go at the lobster platter.

5 The Drover's Inn
MAP F4 ▪ Inverarnan, Loch
Lomond ▪ (01301) 704234 ▪ ££
A flagstone floor, cobwebbed walls
and a menagerie of stuffed animals
to fight your way past – it's quite an
experience. Good ol' pub grub and
amber fluid flow all day.

6 Sheriffmuir Inn
MAP F4 ▪ Nr Bridge of Allan
and Dunblane ▪ (01786) 823285
▪ Closed Tue ▪ £
This middle-of-nowhere former
coaching inn is now a trendy
restaurant well worth finding.
Nothing particularly exotic, but
it's good food at good prices.

7 Starfish
MAP F2 ▪ Castle St, Tarbert
▪ (01880) 820733 ▪ ££
Set in a picturesque fishing village,
this friendly and relaxed restaurant
with local art on the walls serves up
langoustines, lobster, scallops, crab
and other seafood – all of which is
landed daily at the nearby quay.

8 Creagan House
MAP F4 ▪ Strathyre
▪ (01877) 384638 ▪ ££
Winning awards left, right and
centre, this converted 17th-century
farmhouse serves food such as quail
and local lamb, all at surprisingly
reasonable prices.

9 Tigh-an-Truish
MAP F3 ▪ Clachan, Isle of Seil
▪ (01852) 300242 ▪ £
Old-world inn by the famous "Bridge
over the Atlantic"; you half expect
pirates to breeze in. Real ale and
delicious pub grub.

10 Kilmartin Museum Café
MAP F3 ▪ Kilmartin
▪ (01546) 510278 ▪ £
An adjunct of the Kilmartin Museum,
this light-lunch café is mainly
vegetarian but does do excellent
venison burgers, too.

See map on p102

🔟 Grampian and Moray

The northeastern corner of Scotland – a veritable medley of landscapes – is home to equally diverse industries, from the traditions of farming, fishing and distilling to the more recent business of North Sea oil extraction. The high granite massif of the Cairngorms is primed for mountain sports. Then comes the

forested splendour of Royal Deeside, Queen Victoria's beloved retreat, and the quilted fields of Buchan's rich farmland. Along the River Spey is the heartland of whisky production, while on the coast are beaches, cliffs and enchanting fishing villages.

Aberdeen University

1 Aberdeen

MAP D6 ■ Satrosphere: 179 Constitution St; (01224) 640340 ■ Provost Skene's House, Guestrow: (01224) 641086 ■ Maritime Museum, Shiprow: (01224) 337700 ■ Art Gallery, Schoolhill: (01224) 523700

The "Granite City" has beautiful buildings, year-round floral displays and a long beach fringed with entertainments, including the Beach Leisure Centre (see p65) and the Satrosphere, a science discovery complex. Provost Skene's House (once home to a 17th-century provost, or mayor, of Aberdeen) is the oldest building, dating from 1545, while Marischal College is one of the world's largest granite edifices. The Maritime Museum (charting the nautical world from shipbuilding to shipwrecks) is outstanding, as is the Art Gallery, which mixes temporary contemporary shows with a permanent collection spanning the 18th–20th centuries.

AREA MAP OF GRAMPIAN AND MORAY

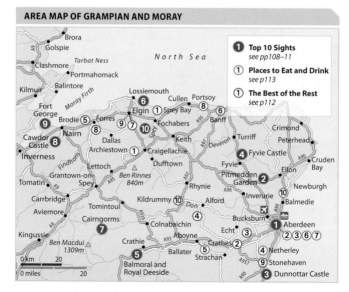

Top 10 Sights
see pp108–11

Places to Eat and Drink
see p113

The Best of the Rest
see p112

The meticulously landscaped Great Garden, Pitmedden Garden

2 Pitmedden Garden

MAP D6 ■ Ellon ■ (0844) 493 2177 ■ Grounds: daily; Visitor centre: May–Sep: 10am–5:30pm daily ■ Adm

The striking patterns and symmetry of the formal Great Garden is like no other. Also here are idyllic pond and wildlife gardens, and a Museum of Farming Life (see p55).

3 Dunnottar Castle

MAP E6 ■ Nr Stonehaven ■ (01569) 762173 ■ Apr–Sep: 9am–6pm daily; Oct–Mar: 10am–3pm daily ■ Adm

Few castles can match Dunnottar's magnificent setting – it stands heroically isolated on a rock – and few castles have endured such intense bombardments. In 1651, while harbouring the Scottish regalia (which were secretly smuggled out by a brave woman), it withstood an eight month siege by the English. Its dungeons, too, have witnessed exceptional sufferings and deaths. Some 800 years of attack have taken their toll, but Dunnottar remains an almost mythical sight.

4 Fyvie Castle

MAP D6 ■ Nr Turriff ■ www.nts. org.uk ■ Castle: Apr–May & Oct: noon–5pm Sat–Wed (daily in Jun & Sep); Jul & Aug: 11am–5pm daily; Garden: 9am–sunset daily ■ Adm

Dating from 1390, this formidable building, and once home of Charles I, is one of the finest examples of Scottish Baronial architecture. Its life through the ages is testified to by the mix of contemporary panelling, 17th-century plasterwork and treasure trove of collectable paintings, arms and armour. The restored 19th century Victorian walled garden specializes in Scottish fruit and vegetables.

Fyvie Castle

Balmoral Castle, the Queen's summer residence in Royal Deeside

5 Balmoral and Royal Deeside

MAP D5 ▪ (01339) 742534
▪ www.balmoralcastle.com
▪ Apr–Jul: 10am–5pm daily ▪ Adm

Queen Victoria bought this castle – her "dear paradise" – in 1852. Balmoral, bordering the salmon pools of the River Dee, remains the holiday home of the monarch to this day and, consequently, the rolling countryside around the banks of the river has taken on the royal moniker. Cast an eye round the castle's sumptuous ballroom, then make the most of the enchanting forest walks.

6 Moray Coast Villages

MAP C5–6

These charming communities thrived in the herring boom of the 19th century, but today only Lossiemouth, Buckie (with its excellent Drifter Museum), Macduff and Fraserburgh continue as fishing ports. For many visitors, Crovie (pronounced "crivie") is the pick of the bunch. Access from the car park is by foot only, its picturesque street strung out below the cliffs – it truly is a fabulous setting. The walk to Gardenstown is an adventure for the sure-footed. Findhorn – famous for its spiritual community – is beautifully located on a sandy lagoon. A self-drive tour of the coastal road (highly recommended) will reveal a dozen other villages, each one possessing its own unique character.

Crovie village, Moray Coast

VICTORIA AND ALBERT'S BALMORAL

It was the riverside setting that Victoria fell for in 1848 when she first visited Balmoral. And it was her husband Albert who worked with the Aberdeen-born architect William Smith to create the white granite palace that replaced the old castle and stands here still, a medley of fantastical turrets typical of the Baronial style.

7 Cairngorms

A superb range of mountain peaks surrounded by pine forests and lochs. Ideal for testing walks, lively watersports and inspiring scenery (see pp34–5).

8 Cawdor Castle

MAP D4 ▪ Nr Nairn ▪ www. cawdorcastle.com ▪ (01667) 404401 ▪ May–Sep: 10am–5:30pm daily ▪ Adm

A private home, handed down through the generations since the time when Macbeth lived here … or so legend has it. Cawdor Castle is full of history and delight, with creepy relics, magnificent trees and a garden maze (see also p43).

9 Fort George

MAP D4

On a peninsula jutting into the Moray Firth is this vast fort complex, built at enormous expense 250 years ago and still used as an army barracks today. Impressive defences now guard a vintage armoury. Check out the special summer events (see p29).

10 The Whisky Trail

Seven of Scotland's finest malt whisky distilleries invite you inside. Apart from the magic of the shining copper stills, the once-secretive process of whisky-making is revealed, enthusiasm infused and the precious uisge beatha ("water of life") consumed (see p35).

A DAY'S DRIVING TOUR

▶ MORNING

Leave **Aberdeen** around 9am and drive on the A93 through Deeside's splendid scenery to Crathie, where you'll find **Balmoral Castle** opening its gates. If, however, you're outside Balmoral's short opening season, then visit **Crathes Castle** or **Drum Castle** instead – less famous, but equally impressive (see p112).

Return to **Ballater**, which you passed through on the way, but take the B976 on the south of the river. The **Station Restaurant** does all-day meals, anything from a bacon sandwich or pain au chocolat to a three-course meal.

AFTERNOON

While browsing the shops in Ballater, look out for royal insignias: they indicate the Queen's favourite establishments.

From Ballater find the A939 and drive north on a twisting road. The terrain is wild, heathery moorland and mountainous. The road takes you past quaint and lonely **Corgarff Castle**, and on to **Tomintoul**, one of the highest villages in Scotland. From here, take the B9008 to the distillery of **Glenlivet** for a tour of their whisky-making vats, stills and barrels, and a tasting. Tours last about 40 minutes; the tastings, unfortunately, much less.

Spend the night around **Dufftown** or **Keith** and plan to drive to **Portsoy** on the coast road either east or west the next day. The tour is about 150 km (90 miles) in total.

See map on p108

The Best of the Rest

1 Moray Firth Dolphins
MAP D4 ■ Info Centre: (01343) 820339 ■ Boat trips from Inverness: (07703) 168097/(07544) 800620

This is the only known resident population of bottlenose dolphins in the North Sea. The aquatic mammals number around 130.

2 Crathes Castle
MAP D6 ■ Banchory ■ (0844) 493 2166 ■ Apr–Oct: daily; Nov–Mar: Sat & Sun; Grounds: all year

Another exemplary 16th-century tower house, with original features in the Great Hall. Wonderful topiary and plant sales from Easter to October.

3 Drum Castle
MAP D6 ■ Nr Banchory ■ (0844) 493 2161 ■ Apr–Sep: Thu–Sun (daily Jul & Aug) Oct–Mar: Sat & Sun; Grounds: all year

One of the three oldest surviving tower houses in Scotland. Its High Hall has been unchanged since medieval times. It was also owned by one family for 653 years.

4 Craigievar Castle
Apr–Sep; Grounds: all year

A delicate tower house with the detail of porcelain. Scottish Baronial style at its best, and with some lovely monkey-puzzle trees in the grounds (see p43).

Craigievar Castle

5 Brodie Castle
MAP D4 ■ Forres, nr Nairn ■ (0844) 493 2156 ■ Apr–Oct; Grounds: all year

Majestic Z-Plan tower house, which has survived many attacks and contains a treasury of furniture and paintings. In spring 400 species of daffodils are in bloom.

6 Duff House Gallery
MAP C6 ■ Banff ■ (01261) 818181 ■ www.duffhouse.org.uk ■ Nov–Mar: 11am–4pm Thu–Sun; Apr–Oct: 11am–5pm daily

Housed in an exquisite Georgian mansion, the collection includes works by Scottish greats Ramsay and Raeburn, as well as El Greco.

7 Elgin Cathedral
MAP C5 ■ (01343) 547171

Once known as "the Lantern of the North", this cathedral was burned out of spite by the Wolf of Badenoch in 1390, but its evocative, picturesque ruins still draw a crowd.

8 Dallas Dhu Distillery
MAP C5 ■ Forres, nr Nairn ■ (01309) 676548 ■ Closed Thu & Fri Oct–Mar

When this working distillery closed it was preserved as a time capsule of whisky-making from 1898 to 1980. Beautifully done, and with a traditional free dram!

9 Stonehaven
MAP E6

Quaint seaside resort with a harbour, an open-air Olympic-size swimming pool and a giant, playable draughts (checkers) board. Dunnottar Castle (see p109) is a short drive away.

10 Kildrummy Castle
MAP D5 ■ Nr Alford ■ (01975) 571 1331 ■ Apr–Sep

The once "noblest of northern castles" is now a grandiose ruin. Brilliant in terms of design, it retains many unique 13th-century features.

Places to Eat and Drink

Archiestown Hotel

1 Archiestown Hotel
MAP D5 ▪ The Square, Archiestown, nr Craigellachie ▪ (01340) 810218 ▪ Closed 3 Jan–9 Feb & 23–28 Dec ▪ ££

A Speyside hotel that's popular with fishermen. Its bistro has earned a good reputation, and wild salmon is a regular speciality.

2 Café Drummond
MAP D6 ▪ 1 Belmont St, Aberdeen ▪ (01224) 619931 ▪ £

Go to Café Drummond to sample the best local and international music. The atmosphere is always convivial, and the young and arty crowd ensure a lively atmosphere.

3 210 Bistro
MAP D6 ▪ 210 South Market St, Aberdeen ▪ (01224) 211857 ▪ ££

The downstairs café and bar forms a relaxing anteroom between bustling Market Street and the upstairs restaurant with its minimalist decor, and harbour views. The menu features fresh and beautifully presented Scottish dishes.

4 Crynoch Restaurant
MAP E6 ▪ Lairhillock Inn, Netherley, Stonehaven ▪ (01569) 730001 ▪ www.lairhillock.co.uk ▪ ££

Rustic decor and a Bavarian chef delivering modern cuisine with flair. Specialities such as venison with fresh local chanterelles or grilled wood pigeon salad grace the menu.

5 At the Sign of the Black Faced Sheep
MAP D5 ▪ Ballater Rd, Aboyne ▪ (01339) 887311/(01224) 860600 ▪ ££

Emporium with an upmarket coffee shop serving interesting sandwiches, sun-dried tomato scones, seafood platters, daily specials and great cakes.

6 Silver Darling
MAP D6 ▪ Pocra Quay, Aberdeen ▪ (01224) 576229 ▪ ££

One of the best restaurants in the country, this is a seafood emporium with Aberdeen harbour spread out before you (see p68).

A Moonfish Café dish

7 Moonfish Café
MAP D6 ▪ 9 Correction Wynd, Aberdeen ▪ (01224) 644166 ▪ ££

Tucked away in a lane, this place is known for some of Aberdeen's most inventive fare.

8 The Shore Inn
MAP C5 ▪ 49 Church St, Portsoy ▪ (01261) 842831 ▪ £

An ale house with atmosphere, right by the harbour. Bar food all day in summer and at weekends in winter. This is where the locals eat and drink.

9 Mansion House
MAP C5 ▪ The Haugh, Elgin ▪ (01343) 548811 ▪ ££

Country club with fine-dining restaurant and casual bistro; both menus feature fresh local produce.

10 Cock and Bull
MAP D6 ▪ Ellon Rd, Balmedie ▪ (01358) 743249 ▪ ££

Rustic meets trendy in this blend of country inn and contemporary gastro-pub. Try the Aberdeen Angus burger.

See map on p108

TOP10 The Highlands

The name alone evokes thoughts of mountains, heather, bagpipes, castles, clans, romance and tragedy. And, indeed, the Highlands have it all. It is the combination of peerless scenery, enduring traditions and nostalgia (albeit for a rather idealized past) that gives the Highlands their irresistible allure. True, the weather is not always great, but rain brings out the best in waterfalls. It's a sparsely inhabited region,

Memorial Cairn, Culloden Battlefield

where you may still find single-track roads and more sheep than people. Life takes on a slower pace, and often hotels and restaurants work shorter hours, but the great compensation is peace. Little wonder that so many aspects of the Highlands have been adopted as symbols of the nation as a whole.

AREA MAP OF THE HIGHLANDS

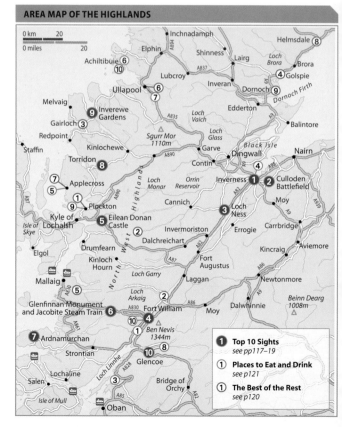

1 Top 10 Sights
see pp117–19

1 Places to Eat and Drink
see p121

1 The Best of the Rest
see p120

Previous pages Dunnottar Castle, Aberdeenshire

Castle Wynd, Inverness

1 Inverness

MAP D4 ■ Tourist Info: (01463) 252401 ■ Museum & Gallery: Castle Wynd; Open Tue–Sat; Adm ■ Inverness Leisure: Bught Lane; (01463) 667500; Open daily; Adm

A fast-growing city with a small-town feel, Inverness is redeemed from the blight of its shamefully dull modern architecture by the majestic red sandstone castle (now the court house), fine old houses and the beauty of the River Ness. Inverness Museum and Art Gallery invites "hands on the Highland Heritage" (but you have to leave the artifacts behind), and Inverness Leisure is a fun-packed swimming centre. The Islands Walk is sublimely peaceful.

2 Culloden Battlefield

MAP D4 ■ Visitor Centre: (0844) 493 2159 ■ www.nts.org.uk ■ Nov–Mar: 10am–4pm daily; Apr–Oct: 9am–5:30pm daily (to 6pm Jun–Aug) ■ Adm

16 April 1746 – the last battle to take place on British soil and defeat for Bonnie Prince Charlie and the Jacobites (see p38). The slaughter by the "Bloody Butcher's" (the Duke of Cumberland's) Hanoverian army was quick and brutal. The battlefield is gradually being restored to its appearance at the time of the bloodshed. To walk here among the graves of the clans is still a peculiarly emotional experience. The Memorial Cairn, which was erected here in 1881, stands 6 m (20 ft) high. The story is well illustrated in the visitor centre.

3 Loch Ness

MAP D4

Ice Age glaciers gouged out a deep trench along a split in the land mass of Scotland, and the resulting valley is known today as the Great Glen. Loch Ness is its *cause célèbre*, with arresting views, the mystery of its reclusive monster and the evocative ruins of Urquhart Castle. Do not eschew a visit to the great loch (see pp28–9).

4 Ben Nevis and Fort William

MAP E3 ■ Tourist Info: (01397) 703781 ■ West Highland Museum: Open Mar–Dec ■ Treasures of the Earth: Open year-round

Britain's highest mountain is 1,344 m (4,408 ft) high and offers a great walk in good conditions (see p46). But the peak is frequently shrouded in mist, and the drive up Glen Nevis offers a more reliable reward, taking you to a lovely waterfall. Fort William lies below the mountain and is a major shopping town with plenty of attractions (see p28). Its West Highland Museum has many Jacobite relics, and Treasures of the Earth exhibits glittering heaps of gems.

Ben Nevis behind Fort William

5 Eilean Donan Castle
MAP D3
- www.eileandonancastle.com
- Feb–Dec: 10am–4pm daily (to 6pm Mar–Oct) ■ Adm ■ Visitor centre: (01599) 555202

No one manages to drive past this castle without leaping for their camera. The restored 13th-century fortress of Clan Macrae stands on a picturesque island on the road to Skye *(see also p43)*.

6 Glenfinnan Monument and Jacobite Steam Train
MAP E3 ■ Visitor centre: (0844) 493 2221; Apr–Oct: 10am–5pm daily; Adm ■ Jacobite Steam Train (01524) 732100; May–Oct

Another memorial to the Jacobite uprising led by Bonnie Prince Charlie *(p38)*, this time on the site where his campaign began. Here, a visitor centre explains the history. The monument is impressive, but the chief attraction is getting here – the scenery en route is stunning. Take time to marvel at the nearby viaduct (featured in the Harry Potter films) and wait for a passing steam train – even better, be in a passing steam train.

Glenfinnan Monument

RETURN OF THE BONNIE PRINCE

Set on reclaiming the British Crown for the Stuart line, Bonnie Prince Charlie landed on the west coast of Scotland in 1745 with but a handful of men. His temerity, as well as widespread support for the Jacobite cause, won over many Scots, and when he came to raise his standard at Glenfinnan, numbers swelled as clans such as the Camerons rallied to his side.

7 Ardnamurchan
MAP E2 ■ Natural History Centre: (01972) 500209; www.ardnamur channannaturalhistorycentre. co.uk; Apr–Oct: 10am–5pm daily; Nov–Mar: 10:30am–4pm Tue–Fri

This peninsula – with its rugged mountains, pretty villages and what is one of the most delightful roads in the country, ending in a parade of white sand – is as lyrical in nature as it is in name. Acharacle is a famed den of musicians, while Glenmore is home to a Natural History Centre with a "living building". Wild deer sometimes graze on its roof. From Kilchoan you can catch a ferry to Tobermory on Mull.

Camas nan Geall, Ardnamurchan

Torridon Hills, near Torridon village

8 Torridon

MAP D3 ■ Countryside Centre: (0844) 493 2229; Apr–Sep: 10am–5pm Sun–Fri; Adm ■ www.nts.org.uk

Just when you think the scenery can't get any better, you come to the Torridon Hills. Flanked by a long sea loch, the red sandstone buttresses of Beinn Alligin, Ben Dearg, Liathach (the highest, see p47) and Beinn Eighe rise up into arresting outlines. From Little Diabaig you can walk a delightful coastal path to Alligin Shuas, or to Craig. The National Trust for Scotland runs an informative Countryside Centre with nearby herds of red deer and Highland cattle.

9 Inverewe Gardens

MAP C3
■ Nr Poolewe
■ (0844) 493 2225
■ Apr–Oct: 10am–5pm daily; Nov–Mar: 10am–3pm daily ■ Adm

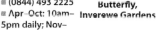

Butterfly, Inverewe Gardens

The sheer richness and variety of plant life growing in what many consider to be a cold wilderness is a tribute to a plant enthusiast's vision and hard work, nature's bounty and the surprising benign effects of warm Atlantic winds (see p55).

10 Glencoe

A rugged mountain range gathered into gorgeous scenery through which the twisting main road seems to creep submissively. A favourite skiing, mountaineering and walking area, and infamous for the terrible 1692 massacre of Clan MacDonald (see pp30–31).

A HIGHLAND DAY TRIP

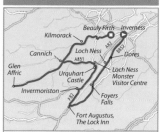

▶ MORNING

Pack a picnic in Inverness (see p117). There are lots of marvellous picnicking possibilities on this route, so it would be a shame not to take one.

Leave Inverness by 10am, taking the B852 to Dores and driving along the south side of Loch Ness (see p117) – a beautiful and much quieter road than that on the northern shore. Try to stop off at the Foyers Falls (see p66).

Enjoy the hill-country drive to Fort Augustus, and pop in for a coffee at the bustling Lock Inn, right beside the canal. Walk along the canal to view Loch Ness from the shore behind the old abbey.

Drive along the A82 on the north side of Loch Ness (stop at Invermoriston to view the river pools and old bridge) and visit Urquhart Castle (see p29). Have your picnic lunch here.

AFTERNOON

Having recharged your batteries sufficiently, visit one of the Loch Ness Monster visitor centres in Drumnadrochit – fascinating, and rather persuasive.

Refill your thermos in Drumnadrochit, then take the A831 to Cannich, and the minor road to Glen Affric (see p120).

Enjoy an hour's walk in this renowned beauty spot, before returning to the bustle of Inverness via Kilmorack and the south shore of the Beauly Firth. The entire round trip is about 185 km (115 miles).

See map on p116

The Best of the Rest

Pretty village of Plockton

1 Plockton
MAP D3

Prime candidate for the title of Scotland's prettiest west coast village, Plockton has sea, palm trees and a Rare Breeds Farm.

2 Glen Affric
MAP D3

Glen Affric is an example of nature's outstanding beauty, most easily accessed from the east at Cannich. At the western end, near Morvich, there's a walk to the breathtaking Falls of Glomach *(see p28)*.

3 Gairloch Heritage Museum
MAP C3 ■ Achtercairn ■ (01445) 712287 ■ www.gairloch heritagemuseum.org ■ Apr–Oct ■ Adm

A leader of its kind, this local exhibition excels with a programme of old-industry demonstrations, such as spinning, corn-milling and butter-churning. By so doing, the museum brings history back into the life of the present. Terrific fun!

4 Dunrobin Castle
MAP C4 ■ Golspie ■ (01408) 633177 ■ Apr–mid-Oct ■ Adm

A home befitting its wealthy landowners, the dukes of Sutherland. Towers, turrets and a palatial interior upon which no expense has been spared. Garden falconry displays too.

5 The Hydroponicum, Achiltibuie
MAP C3 ■ (01854) 622202 ■ www. thehydroponicum.com ■ Apr–Oct: 11am–1pm & 2–4pm Mon–Fri ■ Adm

You'll be amazed at what's grown in the glasshouse here *(see p55)*

6 Ullapool
MAP C3

Delightful grid-plan village with Gaelic street names, boat trips, ferries to the Western Isles, a museum and the dream-world Assynt Mountains. Visit Corrieshalloch Gorge en route.

7 The Road to Applecross
MAP D2

To get to this small coastal village, you'll drive on pure adrenaline – the road climbs 750 m (2,000 ft) in steep zigzags to the Pass of the Sheep. Even they have to hold on tight. The scenery – with views across to Isle of Skye – is magnificent, and from here the more gradual descent into Applecross begins.

8 Timespan
MAP C5 ■ Helmsdale ■ (01431) 821327 ■ www.timespan.org.uk ■ Adm

Well worth a visit to understand the effect of the 19th-century Clearances, which even today is visible throughout the north.

9 Dornoch Cathedral
MAP C4

Madonna chose it for her wedding and 16 earls of Sutherland requested it for their burials; Dornoch is an impressive 13th-century cathedral (now the parish church).

10 Loch Morar
MAP E3
■ www.lochmorar.org.uk

This enormous loch is 12 miles (18 km) long and offers great fishing, walking and wildlife watching – otters, sea eagles and golden eagles, and its own monster, Morag.

Places to Eat and Drink

1 Inverlochy Castle
MAP E3 ■ Torlundy, Fort William ■ (01397) 702177 ■ £££
Many culinary awards have been bestowed upon the restaurant of this prestigious hotel. It boasts three dining rooms, a lavish set menu (of modern British cuisine) and a lengthy wine list.

2 Old Pines
MAP E3 ■ Spean Bridge ■ (01397) 712324 ■ ££
Conscientiously organic, devoted to sourcing local ingredients and a member of the "slow food" movement, this little restaurant has earned a big name.

3 Airds Hotel
MAP E3 ■ Port Appin, Appin ■ (01631) 730236 ■ £££
A country hotel restaurant with crisp, white table linen and candlelight, and a reputation for serving the best of Scottish produce *(see also p69)*.

4 The Mustard Seed
MAP D4 ■ 16 Fraser St, Inverness ■ (01463) 220220 ■ ££
With its stylish interior and riverside location, the Mustard Seed produces some of the finest modern Scottish cuisine in the Highlands.

5 Applecross Inn
MAP D2 ■ Applecross, Wester Ross ■ (01520) 744262 ■ ££
Spectacularly located beyond Britain's highest mountain pass, this pub overlooks Isle of Skye. Local seafood is served, and there is also live music some evenings.

6 Summer Isles Hotel
MAP C3 ■ Achiltibuie, Ross-shire ■ (01854) 622282 ■ ££
A no-choice set menu "strives for perfection" and frequently succeeds at Summer Isles Hotel. Advance bookings only, and vegetarian dishes by arrangement. Gourmet dining in a spectacular setting.

PRICE CATEGORIES
For a three-course meal for one with half a bottle of wine (or equivalent meal), taxes and extra charges

£ under £30   ££ £30–60   £££ over £60

7 The Ceilidh Place
MAP C3 ■ 14 West Argyle St, Ullapool ■ (01854) 612103 ■ ££
Hotel-restaurant-bar and vibrant entertainment venue. Everything from a snack to a feast, plus live music and dance aplenty.

8 Clachaig Inn
MAP E3 ■ Glencoe ■ (01855) 811252 ■ www.clachaig.com ■ £
A legendary haunt of walkers, this hotel offers a wide range of food but is best known for its bar – Clachaig Inn is as essential to Highland trekkers as a first Munro.

9 Plockton Shores
MAP D3 ■ 30 Harbour St, Plockton ■ (01599) 544263 ■ ££
The fruits of the west coast are served up with love and aplomb, on the shores of beautiful Loch Carron.

10 Crannog Seafood Restaurant
MAP E3 ■ Town Pier, Fort William ■ (01397) 705589 ■ www.crannog.net ■ ££
Fresh seafood, a panoramic loch view and generous helpings. The atmosphere is warm and welcoming, and the service efficient.

Crannog Seafood Restaurant

See map on p116

TOP10 West Coast Islands

More than 600 islands lie scattered along Scotland's Atlantic coastline, from seabird-clustered eyots to the landmasses of Skye, Mull, Lewis and Harris. The West Coast Islands represent escapism at its best and amply repay the effort of reaching them with the distinctive lifestyles and hospitality of island folk. Regular ferries run all year, and special "island-hopping" fares are available.

Celtic cross, Islay

1 Islay
MAP F2–G2
■ Tourist info: (01496) 305165

A thriving island with eight distilleries producing peaty malts (see p60–61). Bowmore, the island's capital, has an unusual circular church, designed to deprive the devil of corners in which to hide. Britain's most impressive 8th-century Celtic cross can be found at Kildalton. More than 250 species of birds have been spotted on Islay's varied landscapes.

2 Jura
MAP F2
■ Tourist info: (01496) 820601

The wildest and least visited of all the Hebridean islands. Overrun by red deer and dominated by its central hills, the Paps, Jura has been little affected by modernity: a single road links the ferry port and the main settlement, Craighouse. If you revel in solitude and rugged scenery, the walks are tremendous.

Red deer, Jura

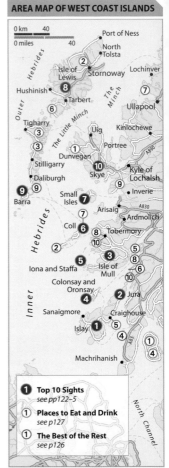

AREA MAP OF WEST COAST ISLANDS

0 km 40
0 miles 40

Port of Ness
North Tolsta
Isle of Lewis
Hushinish
Stornoway
Lochinver
Tarbert
Ullapool
Tigharry
Kinlochewe
Uig
Portree
Dunvegan
Stilligarry
Skye
Kyle of Lochalsh
Daliburgh
Barra
Small Isles
Inverie
Arisaig
Ardmolich
Coll
Tobermory
Iona and Staffa
Isle of Mull
Colonsay and Oronsay
Sanaigmore
Jura
Craighouse
Islay
Machrihanish

The Minch
Outer Hebrides
The Little Minch
Inner Hebrides
North Channel

1 **Top 10 Sights**
see pp122–5

1 **Places to Eat and Drink**
see p127

1 **The Best of the Rest**
see p126

Colourful seafront houses of Tobermory, Mull

③ Mull

MAP E2–F2 ■ Tourist info: (01680) 812377

Matching Skye for beauty if not for size, Mull is the second largest of the Inner Hebrides. Don't miss the prize gardens at Torosay Castle (accessible by miniature railway from Craignure) or the imperious Duart Castle. A tour of the island must include side trips to Iona and Staffa, and Calgary Beach will stop you in your tracks. Tobermory is the place to unwind – its colourful seafront is a classic postcard scene. The Mishnish pub there often has live music.

④ Colonsay and Oronsay

MAP F2 ■ Tourist info: Bowmore, Islay (01496) 810254

Colonsay has provided farmland and shelter to people since at least the Bronze Age, and many of their tombs and standing stones remain. Old traditions persist here, and Colonsay is still a strong crofting (see p124) and fishing community. Wild flowers and birds thrive on this terrain, but it is the coastline, with its mix of sprawling and secretive beaches, that lures most visitors. Check the tides and walk out to the adjacent little island of Oronsay, with its ruined priory; its Christian roots go back as far as Iona's.

⑤ Iona and Staffa

MAP F2 & E2 ■ Boats for Staffa leave from Fionnphort ■ Tourist info: Mull (01680) 812377

Iona is a sparkling island of white-sand beaches with an active crofting community. Visitors come in their hundreds daily in summer to visit the famous restored abbey (avoid 10am–4pm for a chance of peace). It was here that Columba came in 563 to establish a missionary centre (see p38). Staffa contains Scotland's greatest natural wonder: Fingal's Cave, formed by thousands of basalt columns, which inspired German composer Felix Mendelssohn to pen his famous *Hebrides Overture*.

Iona Abbey

6 Coll
MAP E2

■ **Tourist info: Mull (01680) 812377**

Wild flowers, migrant birds, otters, standing stones, active crofts, a castle and a surfeit of beaches contribute to making this a particularly varied and delightful island.

Breachacha Castle, Coll

7 Small Isles
MAP D–E2 ■ **Tourist info: Fort William (01397) 703781**

While Canna and Muck are home to traditional farming communities, Rum was once the private playground of a rich industrialist; you can visit his incredible fantasy home, Kinloch Castle, as well as wander the island's towering mountains. Eigg was a landmark community buyout, and the islander-owners now run a crafts shop and tours. Their ceilidhs *(see p41)* are legendary. The Sgurr of Eigg, a sugarloaf spur, yields fabulous views.

CROFTING

Crofts are unique to the Highlands and Islands. They are small parcels of agricultural land, worked in addition to other sources of income. There are around 17,000 today, and grants now ensure their continuation. But in the mid-19th century, crofters were denied basic rights and suffered great abuse and hardship at the hands of unscrupulous landlords.

8 Isle of Lewis
MAP C2

■ **Tourist info: (01851) 703088**

Although geographically one island, the northern half is called Lewis and, the southern half, Harris. Together, they are world-famous for producing tweed. One thing you absolutely must see in Lewis is the spectacular 4,500-year-old stone circle known as the Callanish Stones, which resonates with a deep sense of spirituality. Arnol has an engaging traditional "blackhouse" (blackened by smoke) and Carloway a fine stone fort. Harris is more mountainous. Driving the "Golden Road" reveals the best scenery; stop at the most spectacular Luskentyre beach, where the miles of white sands and blue-green water could almost make you believe that you are in Australia.

Callanish Stones, Isle of Lewis

Plane on Cockle Beach, Barra

9 Barra

MAP D1
■ Tourist info: (01871) 810336

This small isle encapsulates all the charm of the Hebrides: scintillating beaches, the culture of the Gaels, tranquillity and road-priority to sheep. No matter how you arrive, it will make a deep impression: planes land on the sands of Cockle Beach, while ferries sail into a delightful bay where the 11th-century Kisimul Castle poses on an island of its own. A soothing place to unwind.

10 Isle of Skye
Mountainous, misty and magical, Skye is an island of dramatic scenery, with an ancient castle, an idolized distillery and plenty more attractions (see pp26–7).

TWO DAYS AROUND MULL

▶ MORNING

Leave **Oban** (see p106) on the 9:45am ferry, which arrives on Mull at 10:31am. Book your tickets ahead (0800 066 5000; www.calmac.co.uk).

You might want to spend the day on a wildlife tour, as the island is home to eagles, otters and red deer. Mull Wildlife, for instance, can meet you off the ferry (www.mullwildlife.co.uk). Otherwise head for **Duart Castle**, 13th-century home of the Macleans (a coach service connects with some mid-morning ferries, check with Calmac for the "Duart Excursion"). After exploring the castle and gardens, have lunch in their tearoom.

AFTERNOON

There are plenty of options for walks on Mull or you can drive to **Calgary Bay** to see the stunning white shell beach. Alternatively, make for **Tobermory**, the picture-postcard fishing port that is the island's main town. There are plenty of places to eat and to stay.

MORNING

Set off early to get to Fionnphort, to catch the 9:45am boat trip to **Staffa** (www.staffatours.com, see p123), where you can see Fingal's Cave and the island's famous puffins. You'll be back within 2.5 hours, and can then pick up the quick ferry to the magical island of **Iona**. Visit the abbey, wander its shores and enjoy its serenity. Return in time to catch the last ferry (7pm in summer, but earlier in winter) from **Craignure** back to Oban.

See map on p122 ←

The Best of the Rest

① Arran
MAP G3 ■ Tourist info: (01770) 303774

Long a favourite of Glaswegians, Arran is often described as "Scotland in miniature". Goat Fell is its craggy core, while the surrounds of Brodick Castle offer more forest-path walks.

② Tiree
MAP E1 ■ Tourist info: Mull (01680) 812377

Well-established on the surfers' circuit, this flat island not only boasts some of the finest Atlantic rollers on its beaches but Tiree also claims the highest number of sunshine hours in the whole of Britain.

③ The Uists and Benbecula
MAP C1–D1 ■ Tourist info: (01876) 700286

A string of islands connected by causeways, with huge expanses of beaches on the west and rocky mountains on the east. This is also a wonderful trout fishing area.

④ Gigha
MAP G2 ■ www.gigha.org.uk

An exceptionally fertile island ("Isle of God"), which produces gourmet cheeses and tender plants and flowers, especially in the much-acclaimed Achamore Garden.

⑤ Lismore
MAP E3 ■ Tourist info: Oban (01631) 563122

Situated in splendid scenery, this once important church island is now a quiet holiday retreat. Green and fertile, its name is said to mean "great garden".

⑥ Easdale
MAP E3 ■ Nr Oban ■ Tourist info: (01631) 563122

This former slate quarry has been transformed into a picturesque village. Surrounded by holes and fragmented rocks, it is bizarre and fascinating – a living museum.

⑦ Summer Isles
MAP C3 ■ Tourist info: Ullapool (01854) 612486

The Summer Isles are a small cluster of islands in Loch Broom. They offer solitude and stupendous views of the magnificent arena of the Coigach mountains.

⑧ Kerrera
MAP E3 ■ Tourist info: Oban (01631) 563122

A popular place for yachts to berth, this green, hilly island is ideal for walking, with clear views to Mull and the finest outlook on Oban.

⑨ Eriskay
MAP D1 ■ Tourist info: (01876) 700286

The real-life scene of the *Whisky Galore* wreck in 1941, this is the dream island of the Hebrides. With beaches, crofts, hills – everything is just how the romantic would have it.

⑩ Luing
MAP F3 ■ Nr Isle of Seil ■ Bicycle hire: (01852) 314274

As it is not famous for anything except its defunct slate quarry, you should have this isle to yourself. Pretty, and easy to tour by bicycle. It makes a perfect day trip from Oban.

Lismore Lighthouse

Places to Eat and Drink

PRICE CATEGORIES

For a three-course meal for one with half a bottle of wine (or equivalent meal), taxes and extra charges.

£ under £30 **££** £30–60 **£££** over £60

1 Three Chimneys
MAP D2 ■ Colbost, Dunvegan, Skye ■ (01470) 511258
■ www.threechimneys.co.uk ■ £££

A sublime cottage restaurant in a remote and romantic setting with an international reputation. The excellent cuisine has been rewarded with a Michelin star (see also p68).

2 Digby Chick
MAP B2/C2 ■ 5 Bank St, Stornoway, Isle of Lewis ■ (01851) 700026 ■ www.digbychick.co.uk ■ ££

Bustling, child-friendly bistro by day; candle-lit restaurant by night. Making the most of fresh local seafood and top-quality Scottish steak, book ahead for the good-value early bird menu.

3 Langass Lodge
MAP C1 ■ Loch Eport, Isle of North Uist ■ (01876) 580285 ■ ££

One of the finest dining experiences in the Hebrides. The magical menu takes in the freshest of local seafood, game and beef.

4 Kilmichael Country House
MAP G3 ■ Glencloy, Brodick, Arran ■ (01770) 302219
■ www.kilmichael.com ■ ££

Considering the hotel's five-star rating, its restaurant is a bargain. It has a choice of set four-course menus and a connoisseur's wine list. Booking in advance is essential.

5 Jura Hotel
MAP F2 ■ Craighouse, Jura ■ (01496) 820243 ■ £

Quaint old coastal hotel. In any one evening you are likely to meet most of Jura's inhabitants. Simple food in the scenery of the gods.

6 Scarista House
MAP C1 ■ Sgarasta Bheag, Isle of Harris ■ (01859) 550238 ■ ££

This restaurant keeps things simple with a compact and bijou menu. The locally sourced food is sensational and the view is stunning.

Scarista House

7 Gannet Restaurant
MAP E2 ■ Coll Hotel, Ariangour, Coll ■ (01879) 230334 ■ ££

Waterfront restaurant serving fresh seafood landed on the island. Try the excellent creamy lobster spaghetti, prepared using home-made pasta.

8 The Mishnish
MAP E2 ■ Main St, Tobermory, Mull ■ (01688) 302009
■ www.mishnish.co.uk ■ ££

Celebrated pub on Tobermory's seafront. Always bustling with locals and visitors. Regular live music.

9 Eilean Iarmain Hotel
MAP D2 ■ Isle Ornsay, Sleat, Skye ■ (01471) 833332
■ www.eilean-iarmain.co.uk ■ ££

Charming and cosily set in a huddle of historic buildings by the sea (with its own oyster beds). Highest-quality set four-course menu (three choices for each course) and elite wine list.

10 Café Fish
MAP E2 ■ Tobermory, Mull ■ (01688) 301253 ■ ££

Popular bistro located on the pier where much of its seafood is landed. Produce is locally sourced and the bread is home-made.

See map on p122 ←

🔟 The Far North

Don't let the remoteness deter you, for it is the emptiness itself of the Far North that bestows upon the visitor a sense of wonder and privilege. The dazzling beaches along the northern coastline are a surprise to many, while further north still are the former Viking strongholds of Orkney and Shetland. Orkney's land is green and fertile, and it contains one of the greatest concentrations of prehistoric remains in Europe. Shetland, on the other hand, is a much wilder frontier, festooned with millions of seabirds, and islanders who celebrate their Viking roots with a blazing fire festival, Up Helly Aa, in January.

Great skua, Handa Island

AREA MAP OF THE FAR NORTH

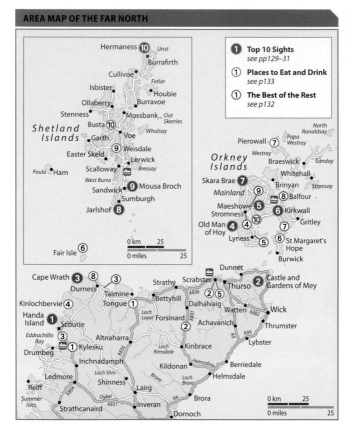

1 Top 10 Sights
see pp129–31

1 Places to Eat and Drink
see p133

1 The Best of the Rest
see p132

1 Handa Island
MAP B3 ■ Information:
(07920) 468572; Apr–Aug: Mon–Sat
Once populated by a hardy people who elected a queen and ran their own parliament, Handa was evacuated when the potato crop failed in 1847. Now it is only a fantastic colony of seabirds that live here. Of particular note are the belligerent arctic and great skuas, kittiwakes, razorbills and the largest assembly of guillemots – numbering 66,000 – in Britain. A ferry from Tarbet will take you to this island.

2 Castle and Gardens of Mey
MAP B5 ■ **A836 Thurso–John O'Groats** ■ **(01847) 851473**
■ **www.castleofmey.org.uk**
On the windswept Caithness coast is the UK's most northerly mainland castle, the Castle of Mey. Since 1952, the late Queen Elizabeth, the Queen Mother, lovingly restored the castle and gardens – her own personal taste is very apparent. The castle and grounds are now in trust for the benefit of the people of Caithness.

3 Cape Wrath
MAP B3 ■ Ferry:
(01971) 511246; May–Sep
This is the most northwesterly point on the British mainland. Perched high on a clifftop stands a Stevenson lighthouse (1827); below, the ocean

Cape Wrath Lighthouse

pounds the rocks in a mesmerizing display of the Atlantic's strength. At Clo Mor, 8 km (5 miles) eastwards, are the highest cliffs on mainland Britain at 281 m (900 ft). The cape is reached by ferry from the Cape Wrath Hotel, and a minibus runs to the lighthouse in summer.

4 Old Man of Hoy, Orkney
MAP A5 ■ Bike hire:
www.orkneycyclehire.co.uk
This sandstone pinnacle rising 137 m (449 ft) from the sea is the most famous stack in Britain. It seems to change colour constantly as the light varies, and never fails to mesmerize. Climbers have scaled its precipitous face. The Scrabster–Stromness ferry deviates to give passengers a view, but its best angle is from land. Hire bikes at Stromness and cycle to Rackwick Bay (on the way visit the Dwarfie Stane, a hollow rock), then it's a 2-hour round trip on foot.

Old Man of Hoy, seen from the easternmost point of Hoy, Orkney

The Neolithic cairn of Maeshowe on Orkney

5 Maeshowe, Orkney
MAP A5 ■ (01856) 761606
■ Apr–Sep: 9:30am–5pm daily; Oct–Mar: 10am–4pm daily ■ Adm

This magnificent stone burial chamber, built around 2700 BC, is a World Heritage Site. Stoop low and walk through the entrance tunnel, carefully aligned with the solstice sun, and enter the greatest concentration of Viking graffiti ever discovered. Norsemen plundered the treasure but left the walls with a wealth of runes describing the kind of boasts and grumbles that people still make today. The torchlit tour is absolutely spellbinding.

6 Kirkwall, Orkney
MAP A5 ■ Tourist info: (01856) 872856 ■ Palaces: (01856) 871918; Apr–Sep; adm ■ Museum: (01856) 873535

The capital of Orkney is an endearing town of twisted streets, ancient buildings and the constant comings and goings of ferries. Most striking of all is the enormous red and yellow St Magnus's Cathedral, built in the 12th century and still going strong. Nearby are the ruins of the bishop's and earl's palaces. The town museum is excellent, and many shops in the city sell an extensive range of Orcadian jewellery.

7 Skara Brae, Orkney
MAP A5 ■ (01856) 841815 ■ Apr–Sep: 9:30am–5.30pm daily; Oct–Mar: 10am–4pm daily ■ Adm

Another World Heritage Site, and one that predates the Egyptian pyramids. In 1850, a storm revealed some ruins in the sands. Archaeologists excavated and were astonished to find a 5,000-year-old Stone Age village, which had been abandoned so suddenly that most of the rooms and furnishings were left intact. Today, you can see the stone beds and sideboards of these Neolithic people, and discover how and what they cooked. A visitor centre explains.

8 Jarlshof, Shetland
MAP B1 ■ (01950) 460112
■ Apr–Sep: 9:30am–5:30pm daily; Oct–Mar: 9:30am–dusk daily ■ Adm

This outstanding warren of underground (but roofless) chambers represents not one but at least five periods of settlement. The oval-shaped houses are Bronze Age; the Iron Age added the broch and wheelhouses; the Picts established their own dwellings; the Vikings erected long houses, and a farm was created in medieval times. This archaeological site, close to the soaring bird-cliffs of Sumburgh Head, is exceptional.

Jarlshof, Shetland

9 Mousa Broch, Shetland

MAP B2 ■ Tourist info: (071856) 841815 ■ Boat trips: (07901) 872 339; Apr–mid-Sep daily (weather permitting)

Around 500 BC the Iron Age people began building defensive forts called brochs. Masterfully designed, these double-skinned walls of dry stones were raised into circular towers, with an elegant taper at their waists. Remains of brochs are scattered across northern Scotland but Mousa is the best preserved. You can only reach it by boat, and then must climb 13 m (43 ft) to the open parapet.

Mousa Broch, Shetland

10 Hermaness National Nature Reserve, Shetland

MAP A2 ■ Unst ■ (01595) 693345 ■ Best visiting times: mid-May–late Jul

When you look from here to Muckle Flugga lighthouse, you're gazing at the northernmost tip of Britain. Aside from the view, the cliff-edged reserve is a favourite breeding ground for bonxies (great skuas). Alongside these pirates (they steal food from other seabirds), there are gannets, razorbills, red-throated divers and a large gathering of tammy nories (puffins).

A DAY ON ORKNEY

▶ **MORNING**

Start the morning from the flagstoned village of **Stromness** (see p132) and head out on the road to **Skara Brae**. The roads turn and undulate on rolling pasture but the way is well signposted – a pity in some respects, as Orkney is a delightful place to get lost in.

You'll need 2 hours to do the Neolithic remains justice, as well as fitting in a visit to **Skaill House** and sampling cakes dripping with icing in the café.

Drive on to the great ancient stone circle known as the **Ring of Brodgar** (see p132), and also visit the roadside standing stones of **Stenness**.

So far you've only covered 20 km (12 miles). Time for lunch over at the **Maeshowe Visitor Centre**.

AFTERNOON

After lunch, take a tour inside Neolithic **Maeshowe**. It's dark inside, and a guide lights up the runes with a torch. Drive on to **Kirkwall**. Visit the cathedral (it has a great little café) and the museum – neither are arduous or lengthy – and walk the town's charming streets.

In the evening, dine at **The Creel Restaurant** (see p133) in St Margaret's Hope and feel like a satiated Viking.

Note, Orkney is also a delightful place to cycle and it's easy to hire bicycles. The car route described above makes a lovely day's cycle ride if you return to Stromness after Maeshowe.

See map on p128 ←

The Best of the Rest

(1) Eas A'Chual Aluinn Fall, nr Kylesku

MAP B3 ■ Take a boat from Kylesku, Mar–Oct: (01971) 502231

Eas A'Chual Aluinn is Britain's highest waterfall. It drops 200 m (658 ft) at the end of Loch Glencoul.

(2) Forsinard Flows

MAP B4 ■ (01641) 571225
■ www.rspb.org.uk
■ Visitor centre: Apr–Oct

The great peatland, known as the Flow Country, offers walks among rare plants, insects and birds.

(3) Smoo Cave, Durness

MAP B4 ■ www.smoocave.org

Remarkable natural cavern beside the sea. You can walk in a little way, but a floodlit boat tour is best.

(4) Pier Arts Centre, Stromness

MAP A5 ■ www.pierartscentre.com

There is an outstanding collection of British fine art here. Most works were created in the 1930s and 1940s by avant-garde artists.

(5) Scapa Flow Visitor Centre, Hoy, Orkney

MAP A5 ■ (01856) 791300
■ www.scapaflow.co.uk

An exploration of the bay of Scapa Flow, where, in 1917, the captive German Navy scuttled 74 ships.

(6) Fair Isle, Shetland

MAP B1
■ www.fairisle. org.uk

Famous for knitted patterns and as a haven of traditional crafts, this remote island has awesome cliff scenery and birdlife (from May to mid-August, puffins are the big draw). The ferry is weather-dependent, so be prepared for a wait.

Italian Chapel, Orkney

(7) Churchill Barriers and Italian Chapel, Orkney

MAP A5 ■ Lamb Holm, nr Kirkwall
■ Chapel: dawn to dusk daily

These impressive causeways were built in World War II by Italian prisoners of war, who were also responsible for the exquisite chapel.

(8) Balfour Castle, Orkney

MAP A5 ■ Shapinsay
■ (01856) 711282

Stay here if you can, but if not at least visit. Guided tours of this delightful home are possible during the summer. They are not offered daily, so phone ahead.

(9) Ring of Brodgar, Orkney

MAP A5 ■ Nr Stromness
■ Tourist info: (01856) 850716

A marvellously atmospheric prehistoric site of 36 slabs raised to form a circle. There are taller (but fewer) standing stones nearby at Stenness.

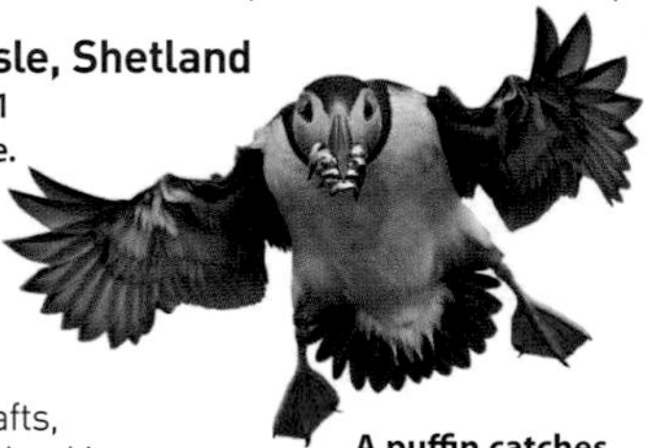

(10) Stromness, Orkney

MAP A5 ■ Tourist info: (01856) 850716

Stromness is a quaint town of flagstoned streets with a museum that draws on the Orcadian connection with the Hudson Bay Shipping Company.

A puffin catches dinner, Fair Isle

Places to Eat and Drink

PRICE CATEGORIES
For a three-course meal for one with half
a bottle of wine (or equivalent meal),
taxes and extra charges.
....
£ under £30   ££ £30–60   £££ over £60

1 Tongue Hotel
MAP B4 ▪ Tongue
▪ (01847) 611206 ▪ ££

A characterful old hotel, the low
prices of which belie the quality of
exotic Highland fare served. The
best of local produce is used with
imagination and flair.

2 The Captain's Galley
MAP B5 ▪ The Harbour,
Scrabster ▪ Open Thu–Sun
▪ (01847) 894 999 ▪ ££

Stylish restaurant in an
exposed-brick former ice
house. Serves a dozen
different kinds of fish, fresh
from the morning's catch.

3 Eddrachilles Hotel, Scourie
MAP B3 ▪ Badcall Bay, Scourie
▪ (01971) 502080 ▪ ££

Among trees on a ragged coastline,
this fine old hotel has a stone-walled
dining room where local smokehouse
food is served. A long conservatory,
too, for catching the sun.

4 Kinlochbervie Hotel
MAP B3 ▪ Kinlochbervie
▪ (01971) 521275 ▪ £

Somewhat stark, but it more than
makes up for it with its good views
and simple value-for-money food.
Hill lamb, venison, salmon and local
seafood are favourites. Good wines.

5 Cups Tearoom
MAP B5 ▪ The Old Chapel,
Scrabster ▪ (01847) 896274 ▪ £

This cute tearoom is set in a tiny
converted chapel on the quay beside
Scrabster harbour. It offers
scrumptious tea and cakes while
you wait for the Orkney ferry.

6 The Creel Restaurant, Orkney
MAP A5 ▪ St Margaret's Hope
▪ (01856) 831311 ▪ ££

Multi-award-winning seafront restaurant in a timeless stone village.
Imaginative cooking with Orcadian
produce – try the wolf-fish broth.

7 Pierowall Hotel, Orkney
MAP A5 ▪ Pierowall, Westray
▪ (01857) 677472 ▪ £

Come here for the best fish and
chips in the isles – probably in
Scotland. Nothing fancy, but simple
home cooking and plenty of choice.

Chocolate truffles,
Cocoa Mountain

8 Cocoa Mountain
MAP B3 ▪ 8
Balnakeil, Durness ▪
(01971) 511233 ▪ £

An unlikely location
for a world-class
chocolatier, but one
not to miss. On
offer are amazing
hot chocolate and
delicious artisan
truffles, as well as a selection of
coffees and teas. A bonus is the
beautiful views of Loch Criospol.

9 Mill Café, Shetland
MAP B1 ▪ Welsdale ▪ (01595)
745750 ▪ 11am–4pm Tue–Sun ▪ £

In this renovated old mill, combine
the visual delights of the Bonhoga
Gallery with delectable snacks:
marinated herring, smoked salmon,
organic quiches – it's all delicious
and praiseworthy.

10 Busta House, Shetland
MAP A1 ▪ Busta, Brae
▪ (01806) 522506 ▪ ££

This historic Shetland hotel also
boasts a revered and reasonably
priced restaurant. The tastiest lamb
on the island is found here, along
with seafood dishes, including
particularly good scallops and
halibut (see also p151).

See map on p128

Streetsmart

Jeffrey Street and the roofs
of Old Town, Edinburgh

Getting To and Around Scotland

Arriving and Getting Around by Air

Scotland has four international airports: **Edinburgh**, **Glasgow**, **Prestwick** and **Aberdeen**. There are also regional airports in Inverness, Dundee, Orkney, Shetland and the Outer Hebrides. Edinburgh Airport is 11 km (7 miles) from the city centre. There are buses every 10 to 15 minutes, which take around 30 minutes, and trams also run to the city centre (35 minutes). Taxis are available too. There are direct flights from the USA and Europe, as well as good domestic links to London. Connecting flights go to Orkney, Wick, the Isle of Lewis and Shetland.

Glasgow Airport is 13 km (8 miles) from the city centre. The best way to get into the city is by shuttle bus (every 10 minutes, journey 35 minutes). Taxis are available too. You can also get a bus to Skye via Loch Lomond and Fort William. There are direct flights from Canada and the USA, as well as good domestic links to London. Connecting flights go to Barra, Benbecula, Campbeltown, Orkney, Shetland, Islay, the Isle of Lewis and Tiree.

Prestwick is 48 km (30 miles) from Glasgow city centre. The airport has its own railway station and trains run three times an hour to Glasgow Central station. Buses run approximately every 30 minutes to the city centre. The airport has links to some European destinations such as Pisa, Rome and Malaga.

Aberdeen Airport is 11 km (7 miles) from the city centre. The Jet Connect bus runs to the city and takes 31 minutes; buses run between 6:30am and 6:30pm. Taxis are also available. The nearest railway station to the airport is Dyce and taxis and buses connect with trains. The airport has direct links to European destinations such as Amsterdam, Paris and Gdansk. There are connecting routes to Orkney, Shetland, the Isle of Lewis and Wick.

Arriving by Coach

Day and night **National Express** services operate out of many major UK cities. Though reliable and much cheaper than trains, journeys are longer. Edinburgh's main coach station is just off St Andrew's Square in the New Town; Glasgow's is opposite the Royal Concert Hall at the east end of Sauchiehall Street. **Stagecoach** overnight sleeper services now run between London and Aberdeen, with stops in Dundee and Perth – the journey takes 10 to 11 hours and is bookable through **Megabus**.

Arriving by Train

St Pancras International is the London terminus for **Eurostar**, linking the UK with the continent. From here there are quick links to Kings Cross and Euston, from where there are frequent trains to Edinburgh and Glasgow.

Arriving by Sea

There is no ferry service between Scotland and continental Europe, but **P&O** sails between Hull and Rotterdam and Zeebrugge, and DFDS sails between Newcastle and Amsterdam. Ferry services by **Stena Line** and P&O operate between the Irish ports of Belfast and Larne to Scotland's southwest coast.

Arriving by Road

The M6, A68 and partially coastal A1 are the main road routes into Scotland; the former for Glasgow, the latter two for Edinburgh. There are no border controls.

Getting Around by Train and Tram

Scotland boasts one of the most scenic railway routes in the world – the West Highland Line, which runs between Glasgow and Oban or Glasgow and Fort William and Mallaig. Book your ticket with **West Coast Railways**. The Borders Railway runs between Tweedbank in the Borders and Edinburgh. A Freedom of Scotland Pass is available on **Britrail**. There is also a **ScotRail** Highland Rover ticket and a Central Scotland Rover. All offer unlimited train travel over a certain number of days. Other train tickets are available through **National Rail Enquiries** and **Trainline**.

Edinburgh has a tram which links the city centre with the airport. It runs along Princes Street with stops at Waverley and Haymarket stations. The Glasgow Subway system comprises a single loop.

By Bus

Scottish Citylink is the largest bus provider, serving over 200 towns and cities. City buses don't give change. Two renowned minibus-and-hostel tour companies are **Rabbie's Trail Burners** and **MacBackpackers**.

By Ferry

Caledonian MacBrayne works the majority of west coast routes. Smaller companies also run ferries to and around Scotland's 99 inhabited islands.

By Car

Driving is the most convenient way to tour Scotland, although parking charges mean that city centres are best explored on foot or by public transport. Roads are of a high standard and there are no tolls. Single-track roads have "passing places". When two cars meet, the car nearest to one should reverse and pull into it, or stop opposite. The Highway Code details all road regulations and can be purchased in bookshops. Seatbelt wearing is compulsory and it's illegal to drive while holding a mobile phone. Scotland has strict drink-driving limits: no more than 50 mg of alcohol per 100 ml of blood. There are car hire firms, including **Avis**, **Europcar** and **Hertz**, at all major airports.

By Taxi

Taxis are regulated and legally obliged to display a licence number. City taxis (**City Cabs**, in Edinburgh, and **Glasgow Taxis**) should be metered but in remote areas unmetered cars operate – ask for the fare before you get in.

By Bicycle

There are 15 long-distance cycle routes and a variety of mountain bike trails on **Forestry Commission** land, plus a number of city cycle networks. Bike transport is possible on most trains, though the faster, long-distance services tend to require pre-booking.

On Foot

With thousands of marked paths, Scotland is a great place for walking.

DIRECTORY

AIRPORTS

Aberdeen
w aberdeenairport.com

Edinburgh
w edinburghairport.com

Glasgow
w glasgowairport.com

Glasgow Prestwick
w glasgowprestwick.com

BUSES AND COACHES

MacBackpackers
w macbackpackers.com

Megabus
w megabus.com

National Express
w nationalexpress.com

Rabbies Trail Burners
w rabbies.com

Scottish Citylink
w citylink.co.uk

Stagecoach
w stagecoachbus.com

TRAINS

Britrail
w britrail.net

Eurostar
w eurostar.com

National Rail Enquires
((08457) 484950
w nationalrail.co.uk

Scotrail
w scotrail.co.uk

Trainline
w trainline.com

West Coast Railways
w westcoastrailways.co.uk

FERRY

Caledonian MacBrayne
w calmac.co.uk

P&O
w poferries.com

Stena Line
w stenaline.co.uk

CAR HIRE

Avis
w avis.co.uk

Europcar
w europcar.co.uk

Hertz
w hertz.co.uk

TAXIS

City Cabs (Edinburgh)
((0131) 656 0830
w citycabs.co.uk

Glasgow Taxis
((0141) 429 7070
w glasgowtaxis.co.uk

CYCLING

Forestry Commission
w scotland.forestry.gov.uk

Practical Information

Passports and Visas

Visitors from outside the European Economic Area (EEA) and Switzerland need a valid passport to enter the UK; EEA and Swiss nationals can use identity cards. Those from the European Union (EU), the USA, Canada, Israel, Australia and New Zealand don't need a visa.

Visitors from other countries should check whether a visa is required at the **UK Visas and Immigration** website or with the British Embassy in their country of origin.

Customs Regulations and Immigration

Visitors from EU states can bring unlimited quantities of most goods into the UK for personal use without paying duty. Exceptions include illegal drugs, offensive weapons, endangered species and some types of food and plants. For information about allowances from within and outside the EU, visit the UK government's website. If you need regular medicine, bring adequate supplies or a prescription with you.

Travel Safety Advice

Visitors can get up-to-date travel safety information from the **Department of Foreign Affairs and Trade** in Australia, the **Foreign and Commonwealth Office** in the UK and the **State Department** in the US.

Travel Insurance

It is advisable to take out an insurance policy that covers cancellation or curtailment of your trip, theft or loss of money and baggage, and healthcare. Emergency treatment is usually free from the National Health Service, and there are reciprocal arrangements with other EEA countries, Australia, New Zealand and some others (check at www.nhs.uk or at www.gov.scot/Topics/Health/Services/Overseas-visitors). A specialist car, medicines and repatriation are costly. Residents of EEA countries should carry an up-to-date European Health Insurance Card (EHIC), which allows treatment in Britain for free or at reduced cost.

Health

No vaccinations are mandatory before visiting the UK. For emergency police, fire, ambulance services, or emergency mountain rescue, dial 999 (or 112). If you need medical help but the situation is not life-threatening, dial the 111 service for advice. These numbers are free on any public phone.

Hospitals with 24-hour emergency services in Scotland include **University Hospital Ayr**, **Borders General Hospital** in Melrose, **Dumfries and Galloway Royal Infirmary**, **Galloway Community Hospital**, **Victoria Hospital** in Fife, **Aberdeen Royal Infirmary**, **Glasgow Royal Infirmary**, **Royal Infirmary of Edinburgh** and **Belford Hospital** in Fort William.

Pharmacies are open during business hours, some until late, and can give advice on minor ailments. Boots is a large chain with branches throughout Scotland, including one on Princes Street in Edinburgh, open until 7pm during the week (8pm Thursday) and until 6pm Sunday.

Hotels are usually able to suggest local dentists and doctors.

Personal Security

Scotland is not a dangerous country, but assaults and muggings can take place. Take sensible precautions: avoid dark, deserted places, use your intuition about entering less salubrious areas and don't flaunt money or other valuables. Don't leave items unattended, especially at airports or railway/bus stations: they may cause a security alert. Women travelling solo should stick to busy areas at night and use only licensed taxis displaying an identification disc. Insure possessions and leave passports and tickets in the hotel safe. Report thefts to the police.

Mountain Safety

If you intend to go walking or climbing in the mountains, be sure you are well prepared for sudden changes in weather conditions; a blizzard can rage on the summit even if the lower slopes are sunny. Check the Mountain Weather Information Service (mwis.org.uk) for conditions before you go.

Have good walking boots, waterproof jacket and trousers, hat, gloves, fleece, map and compass. Also take a simple first-aid kit, whistle, mobile phone and GPS if you wish. Tell someone where you intend to walk and what time you expect to return. In an emergency, contact **Mountain Rescue**.

Disabled Travellers

Visit Scotland *(see p141)* lists all establishments that cater for those with mobility difficulties on their website. Facilities for the disabled vary: modern sights tend to be accessible, but historic buildings may not be – phone ahead to check.

Capability Scotland is Scotland's largest disability organization.

Tourism for All is the UK's central source of disability holiday and travel information.

Disability Rights UK has an annual guide listing accommodation, and runs the National Key Scheme for adapted toilets.

Seagull Trust Cruises is a charity that runs canal boats on the Forth (Edinburgh) and Caledonian (Inverness) canals, specifically designed for the disabled.

Hertz can supply hand-controlled vehicles, suitable for drivers with full upper-body mobility. Disabled parking bays are widespread but you must display an official sign. The AA produce a *Disabled Travellers' Guide* and have a **Disability Helpline** for members.

Can Be Done specializes in holidays and tailor-made packages. Accommodation is wheelchair-adapted, and transfers and private sightseeing tours can be arranged. **Action on Hearing Loss** and the **Royal National Institute for the Blind** both offer useful advice.

DIRECTORY

VISAS

UK Visas & Immigration
W gov.uk/browse/visas-immigration

TRAVEL SAFETY ADVICE

Australia
Department of Foreign Affairs and Trade
W dfat.gov.au/smartraveller.gov.au

UK
Foreign and Commonwealth Office
W gov.uk/foreign-travel-advice

US
US Department of State
W travel.state.gov

EMBASSIES AND CONSULATES

US Consulate
MAP Q2 ■ 3 Regent Terrace, Edinburgh
W edinburgh.usconsulate.gov

EMERGENCY SERVICES

Ambulance, Fire, Police
C 999
C 111 (non emergency)

Mountain Rescue
W mountainrescuescotland.org

HEALTH SERVICES

Aberdeen Royal Infirmary
Foresterhill, Aberdeen
C (0845) 456 6000

Belford Hospital
Belford Rd, Fort William
C (01397) 702401

Borders General Hospital
Huntlyburn, Melrose
C (01896) 826000

Dumfries and Galloway Royal Infirmary
Bankend Rd, Dumfries
C (01387) 246246

Galloway Community Hospital
Dalrymple St, Stranraer
C (01776) 707707

Glasgow Royal Infirmary
MAP V2 ■ 84 Castle St
C (0141) 211 4000

Royal Infirmary of Edinburgh
51 Little France Crescent, Old Dalkeith Rd, Edinburgh
C (0131) 536 1000

Victoria Hospital
Hayfield Rd, Kirkcaldy
C (01592) 643355

DISABLED TRAVELLERS

The AA Disability Helpline
C (0800) 262050
W theaa.com

Action on Hearing Loss
C (0141) 341 5330
W actiononhearingloss.org.uk

Can Be Done
C (020) 8907 2400
W canbedone.co.uk

Capability Scotland
C (0131) 337 9876
W capability-scotland.org.uk

Disability Rights UK
W disabilityrightsuk.org

Royal National Institute for the Blind
C (0303) 123 9999
W rnib.org.uk

Seagull Trust Cruises
W seagulltrust.org.uk

Tourism for All
C (0845) 124 9971
W tourismforall.org.uk

Currency and Banking

Britain's currency is the pound sterling (£), divided into 100 pence (p). Scotland has three banks: Royal Bank of Scotland (RBS), Bank of Scotland and the Clydesdale Banks. Each produces different notes which can be met with confusion or suspicion if you try to use them south of the border, though they are usually accepted. Scottish notes come in £5, £10, £20, £50 and £100 denominations. Coins come as 1p, 2p, 5p, 10p, 20p, 50p, £1 and £2.

There's no limit on the amount of cash you can bring into the UK. Banks tend to offer the best exchange rates and are generally open 9am–5pm Monday to Friday. Some open on Saturday. In remote areas you may find a mobile bank parked and open for business. Bureaux de change work longer hours in the main cities and at airports. They are regulated and their rates are displayed along with commission charges. Cash machines (ATMs) can be found throughout the country. Always shield your pin from view.

Credit cards are widely accepted across Scotland but many small shops, cafés and most B&Bs deal only in cash. Visa and MasterCard are the most commonly accepted cards.

Postal Services

Standard post is handled by the **Royal Mail**. There are post offices throughout Scotland, some in supermarkets or other stores. Larger post offices will open from 9am to 5:30pm on weekdays and until 12:30pm on Saturdays. You can also buy stamps in shops.

Telephone and Internet

Wi-Fi hot spots and Internet cafés are common in the cities. Most towns have cafés with Wi-Fi. The majority of libraries and hotels provide Internet access.

Public phones are easily found throughout Scotland. Some accept credit cards, but others require a phonecard, which can be purchased at many shops. To call an operator, dial 100 or the International Operator (155). For free directory enquiries, call (0800) 118 3733.

When calling a UK number from abroad, dial the access code (0044), then omit the first zero from any standard number. To call abroad from the UK, dial 00 followed by the country code (1 for the USA and Canada, 61 for Australia). Check before leaving home whether your mobile phone will work in the UK. Consider buying a UK SIM card, or use a VoIP service, such as Skype (skype.com). There are still pockets in the Highlands and Islands without mobile coverage.

TV, Radio and Newspapers

Television channels have proliferated in recent years: BBC1, BBC2, BBC3 and BBC4 remain in public ownership, with distinctive broadcasting output in Scotland. Radio stations such as BBC Radio Scotland carry news and travel updates. BBC nan Gaidheal broadcasts in Gaelic.

For current events and news, the free newspaper *Metro* is available at main railway stations. **The Scotsman** and *Scotland on Sunday* are Edinburgh-based broadsheets, while **The Herald** and *Sunday Herald* are Glasgow-based broadsheets. The main evening papers are *Evening News* (Edinburgh) and *Evening Times* (Glasgow). *The Press and Journal* covers the north-east. The main tabloid is *The Daily Record* while *The Sunday Post* has an extremely loyal readership. *The List* magazine is the listings publication covering theatre, cinema, events, bars and restaurants. A range of international newspapers and magazines can be purchased at the international newsagent 351 High St, Edinburgh.

Opening Hours and Holidays

Most shops are open 9am–5:30pm Monday to Saturday. City shops usually open until 8pm Thursday and many now open Sunday, too. Museum and gallery times vary widely, so check before starting out. Last admission to many attractions is 30 minutes before closing. There are three key holiday periods: Hogmanay (New Year), Easter and July–August. The main holidays in Scotland are 1–2 January,

Good Friday (March/April), the first and last Monday in May, first Monday in August and 25–26 December. Local holidays include the "Trades" in early July in Edinburgh, and the "Glasgow Fair", later in July.

Time Difference

Scotland operates on Greenwich Mean Time (GMT) which is 1 hour behind Continental Europe Time and 5 hours ahead of US Eastern Seaboard Time. The clock advances 1 hour during "British Summer Time", spanning the last Sunday in March until the last Sunday in October. In summer, Scotland enjoys longer days than the rest of the UK, whilst the days are shorter in winter.

Electrical Appliances

The electricity supply is 240 volts AC. Plugs are of a three-square-pin type. Buy an adaptor at your departure airport. Most hotels have shaver sockets in the bathroom.

Driving

EEA citizens can drive in the UK, so long as they carry their full and valid licence, registration and insurance documents. Other foreign nationals can drive a car or motorcycle for 12 months, on the same terms. Be sure to get insurance.

Weather

Scotland has a highly variable weather pattern. The east is drier than the west, but rain can occur throughout the year, and heavy snowfalls are possible in winter – seldom longer than a few days, except in the hills. Summer temperatures average 15–22° C (59–72° F); winter temperatures 1–7° C (34–45° F).

The **Met Office** website carries up-to-date, detailed forecasts.

Tourist Information

Visit Scotland provides good general information and has a website – an excellent place to start planning your trip. Visit Britain operates information offices in many cities around the world. Scotland's major visitor information centres are in Edinburgh and Glasgow, and there are regional tourist offices, some open year-round, others open during the summer months only.

Tickets for the **Edinburgh International Festival**, **Edinburgh Fringe** and the **Edinburgh Military Tattoo** can be booked from their respective ticket offices. Many of Scotland's oldest buildings are under the custodianship of **Historic Scotland** or the **National Trust for Scotland**.

DIRECTORY

POSTAL SERVICES

Edinburgh Post Office
MAP N3 ■ 5/6 Princes Mall, Waverley Bridge

Glasgow Post Office
MAP T3 ■ 136 West Nile St

Royal Mail
w royalmail.com

NEWSPAPERS

The Herald
w heraldscotland.com

The Scotsman
w scotsman.com

WEATHER INFORMATION

Met Office
w metoffice.gov.uk

TOURIST INFORMATION

Edinburgh Festival Fringe Box Office
MAP N3 ■ 180 High St
c (0131) 226 0000
w edfringe.com

Edinburgh Information Centre
MAP N3 ■ 3 Princes St
c (08452) 255121

Edinburgh International Festival
w eif.co.uk

Edinburgh Tattoo
MAP N3 ■ 33-34 Market St
w edintattoo.co.uk

Glasgow Information Centre
MAP T3 ■ 10 Sauchiehall St
c (0845) 859 1006

Historic Scotland
w historic-scotland.gov.uk

Hub Ticket Office
MAP M4 ■ Castlehill, Edinburgh
c (0131) 473 2000
w thehub-edinburgh.com

National Trust for Scotland
w nts.org.uk

Visit Scotland
w visitscotland.com

Shopping

Scotland offers a wide range of goods and souvenirs, from local crafts, jewellery and clothing to food and drink. Prices can vary, so it pays to shop around. VAT (Value Added Tax) is charged at 20 per cent. End-of-season sales offer the best bargains, as can outdoor markets, but beware of inferior products. Edinburgh's best-known department store is **Jenners** on Princes Street but there is also a branch of **Harvey Nichols** on St Andrew Square. Edinburgh's main fashion stores are on George Street, while **The Italian Centre** in Glasgow's Merchant City, and **Princes Square** off Buchanan Street, have many high-end stores.

For individual arts, crafts, books and food, make for Stockbridge or Bruntsfield, just outside Edinburgh city centre, or the area around the Byers Road in Glasgow.

Scotland's tartans come in hundreds of patterns and dozens of forms, notably the kilt. These are complex garments to make and require several weeks' work. Tweed for suits, jackets and skirts also comes in a wide variety of designs. Shetland and the Borders are well-known sources of woollens, but there is no need to restrict your search here, as design has excelled in the last two decades. You can visit mills all over Scotland – the **Textile Trail** has details of everything from weavers to kiltmakers.

Packaged food can make excellent presents to take home. Smoked salmon, kippers (smoked herring), haggis, Dundee cake and shortbread are all popular souvenirs of Scotland. When it comes to alcoholic drinks you could take home Moniack country wines, Drambuie liqueur or Edinburgh gin, but by far the most popular drink is, of course, whisky, available in standard bottles, miniatures or special presentation cases. Sadly, it is highly taxed and often cheaper outside the UK. You can purchase it at distilleries, at the Scotch Whisky Heritage Centre and, more prosaically, in supermarkets and off-licences across the country.

It is worth looking out for jewellery in Scotland, a flourishing area of innovative design. Orkney produces an astonishing array of quality jewellery. Some of the more popular traditional designs feature Celtic-knot work and other interwoven patterns, and make use of the Cairngorm, an orange semiprecious stone.

Among companies that produce luxury handmade toiletries in Scotland, **Arran Aromatics** stands out. Their high-quality soaps and creams all use local, natural and eco-friendly ingredients and are well worth trying.

Galleries selling art are found all over Scotland. Edinburgh Printmakers deals in contemporary fine art printmaking. Stills (also in Edinburgh) is a long-established gallery, and Street Level (in Glasgow) is a dynamic photography gallery.

Dining

The choice of culinary options is vast, offering cuisines from across the globe. Italian, Indian and Chinese are perennial favourites with Scots and generally offer good value: Glasgow is famed as one of the great "curry capitals" of Britain. Vegetarians will usually find at least one option on any Indian, Chinese or Italian menu. Glasgow and Edinburgh have the greatest choice of international cuisine and plenty of fine-dining restaurants and pubs serving bar meals and snacks. Set lunches and pre-theatre deals often represent good value.

In the major cities, Scots generally have dinner between 7pm and 9pm and lunch between 12:30pm and 2pm, when pubs, cafés and fast-food restaurants fill up and sandwich bars have queues. However, outside the cities, dinner is generally eaten earlier and last orders for food may well be taken by 8pm in pubs and even hotels and restaurants – check beforehand. It is customary to tip at 10 per cent of the bill, but increasingly service is included in the price.

Restaurant reviews can be found in *The List* and OpenTable, the latter offering online reservations and some special deals. For epicureans, **Taste of Scotland** samples all kinds of places and lists those of a good or high standard, though its listings are not always comprehensive.

It also publicizes food festivals, events and farmers' markets.

Trips and Tours

A ride on an open-top sightseeing bus is a great way to get to know Glasgow and Edinburgh; the best open-top buses allow you to hop on and hop off at leisure. The main operators are **City Sightseeing** and **Edinburgh Bus Tours**. It is also well worth taking a boat trip on the Clyde in Glasgow or on Aberdeen's harbour. **Clyde Cruises** runs a 1-hour Glasgow City Cruise, as well as cruises on the Caledonian canal or around Oban.

Where to Stay

Hotels vary from luxurious country houses to budget chains. Guesthouses and B&Bs offer rooms in private homes with breakfast included. They offer great opportunities for meeting locals. Self-catering flats, cottages, eco-lodges and caravans are cost-effective forms of accommodation for families and groups. Organizations such as **The Landmark Trust** and the **National Trust for Scotland** offer self-catering accommodation in historic properties such as lighthouses and castles. The **Scottish Youth Hostels Association** (SYHA) operates many excellent hostels in Scotland. Take your membership card and travel with a sheet (some require a sleeping bag). There are hundreds of independent hostels with their own websites; no membership is necessary. There's no shortage of camping and caravan sites and they are usually of a high standard and in beautiful locations. Reduced facilities may be offered in remoter areas but the prices will be lower and the views probably even better. **The Mountain Bothies Association** is a charity that looks after over 100 unlocked "bothies" (simple wooden, iron or stone huts). These are all in remote areas and usually have little more than a fireplace, table, seats and a sleeping platform – they are free, but donations are appreciated.

Rates and Booking

If you are planning to stay for longer than two nights in any one place, many hotels, guesthouses and B&Bs will give discounts, as well as offering special weekly rates. You can tour Scotland without reservations but it is generally best to book, especially in high season. The best deals at budget hotel chains are found online well in advance. You can book accommodation at Visit Scotland information centres.

DIRECTORY

SHOPPING

Arran Aromatics
🔲 arranaromatics.com

Harvey Nichols
MAP N2 ■ 30–34 St Andrew Square, Edinburgh
🔲 harveynichols.com

The Italian Centre
MAP U3 ■ 7 John St, Glasgow

Jenners
MAP N3 ■ 47 Princes St, Edinburgh
🔲 houseoffraser.co.uk

Princes Square
MAP T3 ■ 48 Buchanan St, Glasgow
🔲 princessquare.co.uk

Textile Trail
🔲 stla.uk.com

DINING

The List
🔲 food.list.co.uk

OpenTable
🔲 opentable.co.uk

Taste of Scotland
🔲 taste-of-scotland.com

TRIPS AND TOURS

City Sightseeing
🔲 city-sightseeing.com
🔲 citysightseeing glasgow.co.uk

Clyde Cruises
🔲 clydecruises.com

Edinburgh Bus Tours
🔲 edinburghtour.com

WHERE TO STAY

The Landmark Trust
🔲 landmarktrust.org.uk

Late Rooms
🔲 laterooms.com

Mountain Bothies Association
🔲 mountainbothies.org.uk

National Trust for Scotland Holidays
🔲 nts.org.uk/holidays

Scottish Youth Hostels Association
🔲 syha.org.uk

Places to Stay

PRICE CATEGORIES

For a standard, double room per night (with breakfast if included), taxes and extra charges.

| £ under £100 | ££ £100–200 | £££ over £200 |

Edinburgh: Luxury Hotels

Channings

MAP J1 ■ 12–16 South Learmonth Gardens ■ (0131) 315 2226 ■ www.channings.co.uk ■ ££

The decor in this hotel in a wonderfully peaceful setting reflects the Edwardian architecture, while the in-room facilities include Internet access, DVD players and luxurious bathrooms.

Balmoral

MAP N2–3 ■ 1 Princes St ■ (0131) 556 2414 ■ www.thebalmoralhotel.com ■ £££

The most prestigious of Edinburgh's old-school hotels, right on Princes Street, sports two great restaurants, Number One Princes Street and Hadrian's brasserie.

G&V Hotel

MAP N4 ■ 1 George IV Bridge ■ (0131) 220 6666 ■ www.quorvus collection.com ■ £££

Formerly the Hotel Missoni, this eye-catching building is located on the corner of the Royal Mile and is a haven of designer chic, from the fashion-kilted doormen and uniformed staff (clothes by Edinburgh designer Judy R Clark) to the individually decorated rooms (textiles by Glasgow design legends Timorous Beasties).

The Glasshouse

MAP P2 ■ 2 Greenside Pl, Leith Walk ■ (0131) 525 8200 ■ www.theglass househotel.co.uk ■ ££

A private rooftop garden crowns this crystal palace of contemporary design tucked beneath the classical monuments of Calton Hill. Impeccable service, good food and suites with walls of glass, allowing views across the Edinburgh rooftops to the Firth of Forth.

The Howard

MAP M1 ■ 34 Great King St ■ (0131) 557 3500 ■ www.thehoward.com ■ ££

The Georgian character of the Howard extends to the service, too, and every room comes with a dedicated butler to pamper you throughout your stay. The Atholl restaurant is on site for period dining, or have a full à la carte meal served in your room – by your own butler, of course!

The Scotsman

MAP P3 ■ 20 North Bridge ■ (0131) 556 5565 ■ www.thescotsman hotel.co.uk ■ £££

Formerly home of *The Scotsman* newspaper, this solid building has been transformed into a stylish hotel, especially in regard to its leisure facilities, which feature a sleek steel-and-granite pool. Superbly situated, it looks north over the New Town. Bedrooms are well appointed and it has a fine restaurant, Vermilion.

Waldorf Astoria Edinburgh

MAP L4 ■ Princes St & Lothian Rd ■ MAP L3 ■ (0131) 222 8888 ■ www.waldorfastoriaedinburgh.com ■ £££

With its very formal Pompadour restaurant and the Caley Bar for shooting the breeze with friends, the Waldorf (formerly the Caledonian) is something of an institution. Opulence, indulgence and great views at a price.

The Witchery

MAP M4 ■ Castlehill ■ (0131) 225 5613 ■ www.thewitchery.com ■ £££

Champagne and chocolates await each guest in this cocoon of romance. Bose sound systems and cable TV are the modern touches in the seven antique-filled, indulgent suites. It has an excellent restaurant, Witchery by the Castle (see p81).

Edinburgh: Mid-Range and Boutique Hotels

Apex City Hotel

MAP M4 ■ 61 Grassmarket ■ (0131) 243 3456 ■ www.apexhotels.co.uk ■ £

This has joined its sister hotel up the road at No. 31, with modern, simple and functional rooms, and a mix of business and family facilities (photocopying and secretarial services in the former case, cots and highchairs in the latter).

Fraoch House

66 Pilrig St ▪ (0131) 554 1353 ▪ www.fraoch house.com ▪ £
A lovely Victorian building whose period features have been fused with contemporary design to produce a clean and vibrant modern look. Delicious Scottish cooked breakfasts will set you up for a day of sightseeing.

Malmaison

MAP K5 ▪ 1 Tower Pl, Leith ▪ (0131) 468 5000 ▪ www.malmaison-edinburgh.com ▪ £
As its name suggests, Malmaison looks to France for inspiration, and provides a winning mix of good brasserie food and contemporary styling in its rooms – and wonderful bathrooms. Nicely set on the quay, next to Fishers (see p81).

The Bonham

MAP K3 ▪ 35 Drumsheugh Gardens ▪ (0131) 623 6060 ▪ www.townhouse company.com ▪ ££
Run by the same team as The Howard and Channings, The Bonham is the most chic of the three. It has bold styling, with modern furnishings and a range of communication and entertainment devices (including fast Internet and DVDs). The restaurant cuisine tilts towards modern European.

DoubleTree by Hilton

MAP L5 ▪ 34 Bread St ▪ (0131) 221 5555 ▪ www. doubletree.hilton.com ▪ ££
The most style-conscious hotel in Edinburgh. Broad

sweeps of intense colour add vitality to the sharp minimalism throughout, and bedrooms and bathrooms are very well appointed and relaxing. The hotel also has a good restaurant and one of the best bars in town.

Inverleith Hotel

MAP K5 ▪ 5 Inverleith Terrace ▪ (0131) 556 2745 ▪ www.inverleith hotel. co.uk ▪ ££
Victorian town house hotel, close to the Royal Botanic Garden (see p54). Try for the four-poster room, or the Georgian self-catering apartment in the New Town.

Rick's

MAP M2 ▪ 55a Frederick St ▪ (0131) 622 7800 ▪ www.ricksedinburgh. co.uk ▪ ££
You'll find very stylish rooms at Rick's, with the contemporary chic of walnut head-boards paired with angora blankets. Such tactile comforts are complemented by tech ones: DVD players and good sound systems.

Edinburgh: B&Bs, Budget and Self-Catering

Castle Rock Hostel

MAP M4 ▪ 15 Johnston Terrace ▪ (0131) 225 9666 ▪ www.castlerock edinburgh.com ▪ £
Castle Rock is a lively, cheerful and well-run hostel in an excellent central location just off the Royal Mile and below Edinburgh Castle. The large common rooms have a piano and coal fire as well as free Wi-Fi, while a sun

deck provides city views. Amenities include a guest kitchen for self-caterers. Offers dorms, double and triple rooms.

Ibis Hotel

MAP P3 ▪ 6 Hunter Square ▪ (0131) 240 7000 ▪ £
Smart, neat, clean and functional hotel that makes up for in prime location (just off the Royal Mile) what it lacks in terms of space in the bedrooms and bathrooms.

Malone's Old Town Hostel

MAP N5 ▪ 14 Forrest Rd ▪ (0131) 226 7648 ▪ www.maloneshostel. com ▪ £
You can't beat Malone's for location, just 10 minutes' walk from Edinburgh Castle and the Royal Mile. The accommodation is clean and comfortable, and guests enjoy a discount on food and drink in the ground-floor Irish pub. Dorm beds only.

Southside Guest House

8 Newington Rd ▪ (0131) 668 4422 ▪ www.southside guesthouse.co.uk ▪ £
This elegant 19th-century town house with a secluded garden and a library on each landing sports eight beautifully designed bedrooms that would not look out of place in a boutique hotel. Charming hosts provide faultless hospitality that includes free whisky on arrival and a compli-mentary Buck's Fizz cocktail with breakfast.

Tune Hotel

MAP J4 ■ 7 Clifton Terrace ■ (0131) 347 9700 ■ www.tunehotels.com ■ £
This smart budget chain in the West End is located along the tram route. Charges extra for some amenities such as use of a TV, Wi-Fi and towels.

Brooks Hotel

MAP K5 ■ 70 Grove St ■ (0131) 228 2323 ■ www.brooksedinburgh.com ■ ££
Brooks is a reasonably priced, modern, bright and comfortable hotel, in a rustic stone building. In such a compact capital, none of the main sights are very far away, and either the Old Town or Princes Street can be reached within a 15-minute walk. There are TVs in all the rooms, decent beds, uncluttered decor and en-suite showers.

Georgian Apartments

MAP M2 ■ 26 Abercromby Place ■ (0131) 624 0084 ■ www.georgianapartments edinburgh.co.uk ■ ££
For self-catering in style, these two properties in leafy Abercromby Place both have a double bedroom, plus two beds in a screened-off section of the living room, a fully equipped kitchen, free Wi-Fi and free parking. There is a two-/three-night booking policy.

Glasgow: Luxury Hotels

Malmaison

MAP S3 ■ 278 West George St ■ (0141) 572 1000 ■ www.malmaison glasgow.com ■ £
Malmaison exercises its mantra of getting the details right: large, comfortable beds, mood lighting and self-indulgent bathrooms, with power showers and baths suitable for hour-long soaks. There's a French-style brasserie in the crypt (the building is a converted church) and a gym to counterbalance all the lazing about.

Blythswood Square

MAP T3 ■ 11 Blythswood Square ■ (0141) 248 8888 ■ www.townhouse company.com/blyths woodsquare ■ ££
This elegant boutique hotel on a quiet central Glasgow square boasts marble interiors and tweed furnishings. It has a bustling restaurant, a popular bar and a spa.

Hotel Du Vin

1 Devonshire Gardens, off Great Western Rd ■ (0141) 339 2001 ■ www.hotelduvin.co.uk ■ ££
This stretch of Victorian terrace in the West End is the epitome of timeless, sophisticated luxury. The individually styled rooms are awash with deluxe fabrics and carefully selected antique furniture. With opulent bathrooms and high-tech gadgetry in the bedrooms, why venture outside the front door?

Sherbrooke Castle

11 Sherbrooke Ave ■ (0141) 427 4227 ■ www.sherbrooke.co.uk ■ ££
A baronial building in a quiet residential corner of Glasgow close to the Burrell Collection, and an easy 10-minute train ride from the city centre. The decor alternates between an upbeat, boutique look and a more traditional, somewhat stately feel.

ABode Glasgow

MAP T3 ■ 129 Bath St ■ (0141) 221 6789 ■ www.abodeglasgow.co.uk ■ £££
A Neo-Classical 19th-century town house has been given a designer makeover, artfully blending Edwardian wood panelling and ironwork with a modern aesthetic. The rooms are spacious, with big beds and pillows you could easily nest in.

Glasgow: Mid-Range and Boutique Hotels

Alexander Thomson Hotel

MAP T4 ■ 320 Argyle St ■ (0141) 221 1152 ■ www.alexander thomsonhotel.co.uk ■ £
This modern hotel has spotless contemporary standard rooms. It is in a convenient city centre location close to Glasgow Central railway station.

Apex City of Glasgow Hotel

MAP T3 ■ 110 Bath St ■ (0141) 353 0800 ■ www.apexhotels.co.uk ■ £
Behind its curiously angular (and somewhat ugly) glass façade, the Apex offers superb value for money in a very central location. The spacious rooms have pristine facilities and boutique styling. All have Sky TV and free Wi-Fi.

The Brunswick

MAP U4 ■ 106–108 Brunswick St ■ (0141) 552 0001 ■ www.brunswick hotel.co.uk ■ £
Housed in a smart, copper-topped building in the buzzing Merchant City

area, this hotel has a modern-chic interior that is not too formal and a friendly café-bar. The delightful penthouse apartment sleeps up to six and has a spacious sauna.

Ibis Hotel
MAP S3 ■ West Regent St ■ (0141) 225 6000 ■ www.ibis.com ■ £
Like its neighbour, Novotel, the Ibis isn't a prospect that gets the heart racing, but it does provide very good value, achieved through an even tighter economy of scale in the bedrooms and, particularly, in the bathrooms. The location is central, and as a place to take a shower and curl up for the night, drifting off to late-night TV, it's hard to beat for price.

Novotel
MAP S3 ■ 181 Pitt St ■ (0141) 222 2775 ■ www.novotel.com ■ £
While the Novotel is unlikely to feed the mind with recollections of a truly memorable stay, it does the job of providing simple, comfortable accommodation with inoffensive decor. Food and drink are readily at hand in the pleasant bar and restaurant.

Grasshoppers Hotel Glasgow
MAP T4 ■ 87 Union St ■ (0141) 222 2666 ■ www.grasshoppers glasgow.com ■ ££
Squirrelled away on the sixth floor of an office building, this unusual hotel offers affordable luxury in a prime location, right above Glasgow Central railway station. Nice touches include

local art in the corridors, complimentary cakes and coffee, and views across the city rooftops.

Glasgow: B&Bs, Budget and Self-Catering

The Alamo Guest House
MAP U2 ■ 46 Gray St ■ (0141) 339 2395 ■ www.alamoguesthouse. com ■ £
Art, antiques and ornate original plasterwork lend a gorgeous period atmosphere to this 19th-century town house in a prime West End location, just a few minutes' walk from some of Glasgow's top restaurants. Perks include posh toiletries, bathrobes and a movie library, while the more expensive rooms have garden views; the best room boasts a luxurious freestanding bathtub.

Ashton B&B
MAP U2 ■ 27 Ashton Rd ■ (0141) 579 6770 ■ www. ashtonglasgow.com ■ £
A great-value B&B located in the city's lively West End, close to the bars and restaurants of Ashton Lane and with good public transport links to the city centre. The bedrooms are stylish and comfortable, and the welcoming owners are beyond helpful. Cash only; no credit cards.

Glasgow Youth Hostel
MAP V2 ■ 8 Park Terrace ■ (0141) 332 3004 ■ www.syha.org.uk ■ £
Although it's half an hour's walk from the city centre, Glasgow's SYHA hostel enjoys a lovely setting in an elegant

and spacious Victorian mansion overlooking Kelvingrove Park, convenient for Kelvingrove Art Gallery & Museum. Some of the rooms have glorious views.

SACO
MAP U4 ■ 53 Cochrane St ■ (0845) 122 0405 ■ www. sacoapartments.co.uk ■ £
These twelve luxury-on-a-budget one-bedroom apartments in the heart of town offer a minimum three-night stay. They are fully serviced with simple, modern furnishings.

Dreamhouse Apartments
(0845) 226 0232 ■ www.dreamhouse apartments.com ■ ££
In various West End locations close to Kelingrove Park, these luxurious one- and two-bed apartments have elegant modern styling and full maid service. An excellent choice if you're staying for more than a few nights.

Mainland: Luxury Hotels

Culloden House, Inverness
MAP D4 ■ (01463) 790461 ■ www.culloden house.co.uk ■ ££
Bonnie Prince Charlie stayed here (he commandeered the place in 1746) and the hosts have dined out on the story ever since. Glistening chandeliers and Adams plasterwork enhance a building of exceptional architecture. Every room at Culloden House is uniquely decorated, and there's superb dining, too.

Isle of Eriska Hotel, Ledaig

MAP E3 ▪ Ledaig ▪ (01631) 720371 ▪ www.eriska-hotel. co.uk ▪ ££

Isle of Eriska Hotel sees extravagant luxury on an island sanctuary near the mouth of Loch Linnhe. The defifition of good living (see p57).

Boath House, Moray

MAP D4 ▪ Auldearn, Nairn ▪ (01667) 454896 ▪ www.boath-house.com ▪ £££

A Georgian mansion set amid gardens and woodland, this is not just a hotel but also a luxury retreat with a sauna, spa, gym, and a full range of beauty treatments, including Ayurvedic remedies. Good healthy food completes the package.

Cameron House, Loch Lomond

MAP F4 ▪ Near Luss ▪ (01389) 755565 ▪ £££

An enduring favourite to which many stars hop by helicopter from Glasgow. Right on Loch Lomond, this turreted mansion has extensive leisure facilities, including a large pool, tennis courts and a marina. At mealtimes, choose between the three-AA-rosette dining room and the all-day Marina Bar restaurant.

Glencoe House, Glencoe

MAP E3 ▪ Glencoe ▪ (01855) 811179 ▪ www. glencoe-house.com ▪ £££

This lovely 19th-century mansion, built by the governor of Canada's Hudson Bay Company, still sports much finery from the time, including marble fireplaces, parquet floors and ornate ceilings. Service is attentive but not intrusive: breakfast is served whenever you want.

Gleneagles, Auchterarder

MAP F4 ▪ (01764) 662 231 ▪ www.gleneagles. com ▪ £££

A superb country-house resort, arguably Scotland's finest, with warm personal service and old-fashioned style. Leisure activities available at Gleneagles include shooting, riding, fishing and a fantastic spa, not to mention a world-class golf course (see p59). The resort is also home to one of Scotland's best and most famous restaurants, the French-influenced Andrew Fairlie (see p95).

Inverlochy Castle, Fort William

MAP E3 ▪ (01397) 702177 ▪ www.inverlochy castlehotel.com ▪ £££

This has been among Scotland's elite for so long, it has become the benchmark for excellence. The hotel is set against a stunning landscape of surrounding mountains and has sumptuous decor. The King of Norway presented the dining-room furniture as a gift, and he wouldn't be disappointed with what's served upon it.

Kinloch House, Blairgowrie

MAP E5 ▪ Blairgowrie ▪ (01250) 884237 ▪ www. kinlochhouse.com ▪ £££

Kinloch House is the perfect place to enjoy all the key features of a 19th-century Scottish country house. There are individually decorated rooms. Wander in the beautiful walled garden containing hundreds of roses, and explore the dignified public rooms including a venerable portrait gallery.

Knockinaam Lodge, Portpatrick

MAP H3 ▪ (01776) 810471 ▪ www.knocki naamlodge.com ▪ £££

Knockinaam nestles in a romantic setting by the sea. Room rates include top-quality dinner and breakfast (see p89).

Mainland: Mid-Range and Boutique Hotels

Castle Venlaw, Peebles

MAP G5 ▪ Edinburgh Rd ▪ (01721) 720384 ▪ www.venlaw.co.uk ▪ ££

Castle Venlaw is a luxury boutique hotel in an 18th-century Scottish castle. One of the imposing turrets houses the Library Bar with its open log fire and wonderful woodland views. Some of the elegant bedrooms have four-poster beds.

Ednam House Hotel, Kelso

MAP G6 ▪ (01573) 224168 ▪ www.ednam house.com ▪ ££

Classic Georgian mansion looking over the River Tweed – a major draw for its rooms and restaurant. The building itself retains period features and, though the patterns are slightly busy, the clutter of fishing paraphernalia adds a decidedly homely feel.

Fauhope, Melrose
MAP G5 ▪ Gattonside, Melrose ▪ (01896) 823184 ▪ www.fauhopehouse. com ▪ ££

Built in 1897, this secluded house has enchanting views to the River Tweed and Eildon Hills. It is tastefully decorated and staff display impeccable hospitality. The food is excellent, as Fauhope is run by Sheila Robson, restaurateur of Marmions (see p89). For comfort and price, this ranks among the best in the Borders.

Glen Clova Hotel, Glen Clova
MAP E5 ▪ Nr Kirriemuir ▪ (01575) 550350 ▪ www.clova.com ▪ ££

This excellent old hotel offers character and relaxation in spades, in the best of central Scotland's scenery. From a bunkhouse to a four-poster bed, bar snacks to cordon bleu, this establishment offers eats and sleeps catering for all needs.

Glenfinnan House Hotel, Glenfinnan
MAP E3 ▪ (01397) 722235 ▪ www.glenfinnanhouse. com ▪ ££

An imposing 18th-century pine-panelled stately home which overlooks Loch Shiel. Excellent value, the rooms vary in price according to the views. Glenfinnan House has good home cooking and a bar where folk musicians often gather.

Kinkell House, Cromarty Firth
MAP C/D4 ▪ Conor Bridge, nr Dingwall ▪ (01349) 861270 ▪ www.kinkell househotel.com ▪ ££

In a delightful country house, which catches the sunrise over the Cromarty Firth and the sunset over Ben Wyvis, this hospitable hotel is beautifully furnished and decorated. It offers great value, and the tariff includes a fine à la carte dinner.

Old Pines Hotel, Spean Bridge
MAP E3 ▪ (01397) 712324 ▪ www.oldpines.co.uk ▪ ££

This Scandinavian-style hotel in a single-storey house, with easy wheelchair access, has a play area for children and views to Ben Nevis. Dinner at the restaurant (by Chef Ryan Glen) is included with accommodation rates (see p121).

Riverwood Strathtay, Pitlochry
MAP E4 ▪ Nr Pitlochry ▪ (01887) 840751 ▪ www. riverwoodstrathtay.com ▪ ££

A stylish retreat with four acres of lawns and woods beside the River Tay with its good trout fishing. Each room is decorated in a chic and neutral Arts and Crafts style.

Mainland: Guesthouses and B&Bs

Beach Cottage B&B, Inverness
MAP D4 ▪ 3 Alturlie Point ▪ (01463) 237506 ▪ www. beachcottageinverness. co.uk ▪ £

It's not unusual to see dolphins swimming in

the Moray Firth from this renovated 18th-century fisherman's cottage, and rooms have been designed to make the most of the stunning views.

Dalshain Guest House, Pitlochry
MAP E5 ▪ (01796) 472173 ▪ www.dalshain.co.uk ▪ £

A wonderful 18th-century guesthouse set within an acre of secluded woodland and gardens that offer a quiet retreat beyond the fringes of Pitlochry. Rooms are attractive and modern and there is a comfortable guest lounge replete with open fireplace.

Dunure Inn, Dunure
MAP G3 ▪ 17 Harbour View ▪ (01292) 500549 ▪ www.dunureinn.co.uk ▪ £

This harbourside pub just south of Ayr offers a handful of spacious, boutique-style rooms near Culzean Castle (see pp32–3). The restaurant serves international dishes and good-value half-board deals are usually available.

Fiorlin, Melrose
MAP G5 ▪ Abbey St ▪ (01896) 822984 ▪ www. melroseaccommodation. co.uk ▪ £

Close to the abbey and set inside its own walls in a quiet cul-de-sac, this B&B offers very comfortable self-contained accomodation, with shops and restaurants nearby. The owners are attentive to guests' needs.

Glencoe Youth Hostel, Ballaculish
MAP E3 ▪ (01855) 811219
▪ www.syha.org.uk ▪ £
This quiet hostel is situated in one of the most spectacular glens in Scotland, on the doorstep of some of the best year-round walking and climbing. Compare notes with other ramblers at the famous nearby Clachaig Inn, where the day's mountaineering tales are swapped every night.

Glenfinnan Sleeping Car, Glenfinnan
MAP E3 ▪ Glenfinnan Station Museum
▪ (01397) 722295
▪ Jun–Oct ▪ £
The most unusual beds in Scotland are to be found in a disused railway sleeping coach, which now stands at Glenfinnan Station Museum. It sleeps 10, and you can pay by the night or hire the whole wagon by the week. All-day light meals are served in an adjacent coach. All aboard!

Globe Inn, Aberdeen
MAP D6 ▪ 13 North Silver St ▪ (01224) 624258
▪ www.theglobeinn-aberdeen.co.uk ▪ £
The bedrooms here are above one of Aberdeen's best pubs, so this is not a place for early-to-bed guests, but the value and location – bang in the city centre – can't be beaten. Continental breakfast is served in your room. Parking on the street needs to be paid for.

Rowardennan Youth Hostel, nr Drymen
MAP F4 ▪ (01360) 870259
▪ 3 Mar–28 Oct ▪ £
One of the busiest youth hostels in Scotland because of its superb location: on the banks of Loch Lomond and also on the West Highland Way walking path (see p48). Ben Lomond sweeps up at the back and at the front is a private beach. Rowardennan is very popular with families. Definitely book ahead.

Rua Reidh Lighthouse, Gairloch
MAP C3 ▪ (01445) 771263
▪ www.ruareidh.co.uk ▪ £
Built in 1910 by a cousin of Robert Louis Stevenson, this idyllic lighthouse offers some magnificent views over the Minch to Skye and the Western Isles. There are basic private rooms and hostel beds available.

Easter Dunfallandy Country House, Pitlochry
MAP E4/5 ▪ (01796) 474031 ▪ www.dunfallandy.co.uk ▪ ££
In an idyllic location overlooking the Tummel Valley, this small country B&B has just three bedrooms. Enjoy inexpensive rural living, where the day begins with a hearty Highland breakfast. Neither children under 12 nor dogs are allowed, so there is no risk of disturbance to the peace and tranquillity.

Five Pilmour Place, St Andrews
MAP F5 ▪ (01334) 478665
▪ www.5pilmourplace.com ▪ ££
The best of a string of pleasant guesthouses by St Andrews' Old Course, the rooms here have a modern boutique feel, thanks to high-quality furnishings and various comforts.

Guests can enjoy the walled garden. An excellent breakfast is included in the room rate.

Mackay's, Durness
MAP B4 ▪ (01971) 511202
▪ ££
This long-standing family-run hotel has smart wood-and-slate decor in its log-fired lounge, and stylishly decorated rooms. It's welcoming as well as immaculate, and enjoys wonderful views of the surrounding countryside.

Island Accommodation

Berneray Youth Hostel, Berneray
MAP C1 ▪ North Uist
▪ (08701) 553255 ▪ £
A charming thatched cottage, Berneray Youth Hostel provides somewhat primitive accommodation in the most stunning location. Plus it's just four hops to the beach.

Calgary Farmhouse
MAP E2 ▪ Calgary, Mull
▪ (01688) 400256
▪ www.calgary.co.uk ▪ £
Close to Calgary Bay, one of Mull's most beautiful white-sand beaches, this converted farm complex offers a range of beautifully designed self-catering accommodation, from a cozy studio flat for two to the magnificent oak-beamed Hayloft, which sleeps up to eight people comfortably.

Lochranza Youth Hostel, Arran
MAP G3 ▪ Lochranza
▪ (0870) 004 1140
▪ 3 Mar–28 Oct ▪ £
In a beautiful location below Arran's mountains, and close to the sea and

an ancient castle, rests Lochranza Hostel. Secluded in a woodland garden, this old country house makes a great base for exploring the island. It is handily close to a bus route and has its own small shop.

Salen Hotel, Mull
MAP E2 ■ Salen, Aros ■ (01680) 300324 ■ www.salenhotelmull.co.uk ■ £
Centrally located and close to Ben More, this informal hotel offers comfortable rooms and superb views. The dining room boasts panoramic vistas, and there are hearty dishes on the menu. Pets welcome.

Ardhasaig House, Isle of Harris
MAP C2 ■ Ardhasaig ■ (01859) 502500 ■ www.ardhasaig.co.uk ■ ££
Set by one of the most picturesque roads in the isles, this 1904 house has been completely refurbished, while retaining certain period features. With light decor, simple furnishings and captivating views, this B&B is of the highest calibre. There is the option of a four-course set menu for dinner. A self-catering cottage is also available.

Broad Bay House, Lewis
MAP B2 ■ (01851) 820990 ■ Mar–Oct ■ www.broadbayhouse.co.uk ■ ££
Broad Bay House is a beautifully located guesthouse beside a sweeping sandy beach, only a short drive north of Stornoway. The

contemporary rooms are styled in natural wood and have a glut of hi-tech facilities, including iPod docking stations.

Busta House Hotel, Shetland
MAP A1 ■ Brae ■ (01806) 522506 ■ www.bustahouse.com ■ ££
A remote and peaceful country house hotel, this is one of the great get-away-from-it-all retreats in Scotland. Busta House delivers first-class quality in every respect and detail.

The Colonsay Hotel, Colonsay
MAP F2 ■ (01951) 200316 ■ www.colonsayestate.co.uk ■ ££
Built in 1750, this traditional inn has always been an island social centre and often hosts live music. Rooms are bright and simple, and guests can enjoy a garden, terrace and library. Curl up with a good book and enjoy some fine sea views over the neighbouring island of Jura.

Flodigarry Country House, Skye
MAP C2 ■ Staffin, Isle of Skye ■ (01470) 552203 ■ www.hotelintheskye.co.uk ■ ££
Situated close to the sea and below the Trotternish Ridge stands this 19th-century mansion, which retains many period features, including a magnificent billiard room. The views from the sunny conservatory are simply marvellous. Flodigarry Country House is an affordable retreat with a growing, glowing reputation for good food.

Glenegedale, Islay
MAP F2 ■ (01496) 300400 ■ www.glenegedalehouse.co.uk ■ ££
Glenegedale is a classic whitewashed Hebridean house in a glorious setting overlooking Laggan Bay and the Irish coast. Every room here has been individually decorated and there is a full range of modern facilities and quaint touches, such as chocolates left on the pillow, bowls of fresh fruit and roaring peat fires in the colder months. An Cuan, run by the same owners, is another guesthouse located nearby, with spectacular Laggan Bay views from its elevated position.

Holland House, Orkney
MAP A5 ■ (01856) 771 400 ■ www.hollandhouseorkney.co.uk ■ ££
Holland House is a small B&B in a peaceful spot, offering three country-style rooms and a pleasant lounge, conservatory and walled garden. Breakfasts include local sausage, black pudding and home-made preserves.

Viewfield House, Skye
MAP D2 ■ Portree ■ (01478) 612217 ■ Apr–Oct ■ £
A rambling building set in 81,000 sq m (97,000 sq yards) of woodland garden, Viewfield House has been a family home since the early 19th century. Guests are made very welcome and, if they so wish, can choose to dine together in the Victorian dining room.

Index

Acknowledgments

Author
Alastair Scott is a frelance travel writer and photographer based in Edinburgh and on the Isle of Skye.

Additional contributors
Rebecca Ford, Neil Wilson

Publishing Director Georgina Dee

Publisher Vivien Antwi

Design Director Phil Ormerod

Editorial Michelle Crane, Rachel Fox, Freddie Marriage, Fíodhna Ní Ghríofa, Scarlett O'Hara, Erin Richards, Sally Schafer

Design Tessa Bindloss, Richard Czapnik, Jaynan Spengler

Commissioned Photography Joe Cornis Crawfor, Alex Havret, Ian O'Leary, Rough Gui Helena Smith, Clive Streeter, Linda Whitwarr

Picture Research Susie Peachey, Ellen F Lucy Sienkowska, Oran Tarjan

Cartography Reetu Pandey, Suresh Kur James Macdonald

DTP Jason Little, George Nimmo

Production Linda Dare

Factchecker Christian Williams

Proofreader Nikky Twyman

Indexer Helen Peters

First edition created by Blue Island Publishing, London

Revisions Team
Neha Chander, Rebecca Flynn, Rahul Kur Rada Radojicic

Picture Credits

The publisher would like to thank the foll for their kind permission to reproduce the photographs:

Key: a-above; b-below/bottom; c-centre; l-left; r-right; t-top

4Corners: SIME/Olimpio Fantuz 4b.

Alamy Images: age fotostock/Gonzalo Azumendi 61tl; The Archtives 10cl; blickwinkel 7tr, 129r; Blue Gum Pictures 129b; Mark Boulton 30bl; Douglas Carr 32cla, 58b, 107clb; David Chapman 130br; Derek Croucher 26cl; Ian Dagnall 68tl,116tl; Karen Debler 35cra; Dave Donaldson 71tr; eye35 63tr; D. G. Farquhar 66t, 119clb; Keith Fergus 28bl; FLPA 11br; fotostock/Juan Carlos Muñoz /WWE 67tr; Philip Game 98cla; Jeff Gilbert 19tr; Ross Gilmore 74tl; Dennis Hardley 30-1, 47t, 110t, 124cla; Cath Harries 60b, Hemis fr / Rieger Bertrand 11cb, Hemis.fr / Gregory Gerault 118ca; Jan Holm 11tr; Holmes Garden Photos/Neil Holmes 92cb; imageBROKER/Jose Antonio Moreno Castellano 102tr; Imagestate Media Partners Limited - Impact Photos/Peter Thompson 27crb; Brian Jannsen 14t; John Carroll Photography 2tr, 36-7;

John Peter Photography 35bl, 84tl, 86tl, 98b, 104-5; Kayroxby Image Scotland 15br; Look Die Bildagentur der Fotografen GmbH/Andreas Strauss 12br, 69cla; Loop Images Ltd/Cath Evans 125tl; Vincent Lowe 131cl; David Lyons 35tr; Matthew Clarke 52t; Niall McDiarmid 63clb; John McKenna 52cb; Jen Owens 18bl; Paintin / Scottish National Gallery *An Old Woman Cooking Eggs* (1618) by Diego Rodriguez de Silva y Velazquez, 16bl, /Scottish National Gallery/ *A Seascape, Shipping by Moonlight* (1864) Claude Monet 17bl; Dave Pattison 68b; Photoshot 128cra; John Potter 91b; Prisma Bildagentur AG 23tc; M Ramírez 20cr; Rolf Richardson 29bl;

22cra; Ruth Tomlinson 105tl; Andy Trowbridge 132cb; VIEW Pictures Ltd /Hufton + Crow 23bl.

Crannog Cruises and Restaurant: 121br.

Crown Copyright Reproduced Courtesy of Historic Scotland: Santiago Arribas Pena 10ca, 56t, 88tl, 106tl, 130t.

Dreamstime.com: App555 11tl, 66br; Apw 69tr; Jennifer Barrow 11cra, 28-9, 75tl, 76b; Lukas Blazek 4crb; John Braid 34-5; Bukki88 120tl; Cphotography 59t; Creativehearts 108cla; Elxeneize 6cla, 24-5, 26-7, 53tr; Eudaemon 62t; Nicola Ferrari 57ca; Paula Fisher 132tr; Grian12 99tl; H368k742 26bl; Nataliya Hora 4t; Gail Johnson 87cl; Julietphotography 76cra; Holger Karius 126b; Andrea La Corte 13tr; Lowsun 6ca, 117tl; Magsellen 85tr; Daniel Masters 103b; James Mcquarrie 26cb; Meunierd 23br, 96tl; Dmitry Naumov 69clb; Photographerlondon

53bl; Photoprofi30 62bl; Photowitch 124-5bl; Pitsch22 90tr; Adrian Pluskota 4cl; Franco Ricci 4cr; Juergen Schonnop 32-3; Ryan Stevenson 40t; Stevewphoto 30br; Stockcube 4cla; Sueburtonphotography 123t; Petr Švec 12-3, 28cl; Tazufos 31clb; Tonythomas1958 82-3; Andrew Ward 122bl; Weetoonpics 122tl; Ketsiree Wongwan 19tl.

Edinburgh Festival Fringe Society: Jane Barlow 70cl.

Edinburgh International Science Festival: 71bl.

Eilean Donan Castle: 43t.

Fife Coast and Countryside Trust: Richard Newton 49cla.

Getty Images: AFP/Andy Buchanan 39bl; Alan Copson 3tl, 72-3; Ross Gilmore 70tr; Ian Gavan 39tr; Maremagnum 3tr, 44-5, 134-5; Michael Breitung Photography 114-5; Oxford Science Archive/Print Collector 39cla; David C Tomlinson 15ca; Adina Tovy 41tr.

Glamis Castle: 42b, 93clb.

Go Ape: Red Consultancy 64tl.

Highland Wildlife Park: Alex R 34crb.

Inveraray Castle: 105bl.

Isle of Eriska: Dennis Hardley Photography 57crb.

Knockinaam Lodge: 89br.

Landmark Forest Adventure Park: Captivating Photography/Charné Hawkes 65t.

Loch Lomond & The Trossachs National Park: 48t.

Mary Evans Picture Library: Illustration by J R Skelton in Scotland's Story (1906) 38tl.

Moonfish Cafe: 113c.

Moray Council: 48br.

Scottish National Galleries: *Lady Agnew of Lochnaw* (1932) by John Singer Sargent 16tr.

National Museums of Scotland: Andrew Lee 18cr.

National Trust for Scotland: Arduaine Garden 33cra, 55bl; Kathy Collins 33bc; John Sinclair 32bl, 112bl.

Princes Square: 100br.

Royal Botanic Garden Edinburgh: 54t.

Scarista House: 127cra.

Scottish National Gallery of Modern Art: 77tl.

Scottish National Heritage: Becky Duncan Photography 49br.

Scottish Seabird Centre: 65cb.

SuperStock: View Pictures Ltd 10bl.

The Achiltibuie Garden Ltd: Allan Graham 55tr.

The Balmoral: Susie Lowe 81cra.

The Dome: 80bl.

The Peat Inn: Gill Mair 95tr.

Timberyard: 81clb.

Cover
Front and spine - **Corbis:** Christophe Boisvieux
Back - **Dreamstime.com:** Jennifer Barrow

Pull Out Map Cover
Corbis: Christophe Boisvieux
All other images © Dorling Kindersley
For further information see: www.dkimages.com

Penguin Random House

Printed and bound in China

First published in Great Britain in 2003 by Dorling Kindersley Limited 80 Strand, London WC2R 0RL

Copyright 2003, 2016 © Dorling Kindersley Limited

A Penguin Random House Company

16 17 18 19 20 10 9 8 7 6 5 4 3 2 1

Reprinted with revisions 2005, 2007, 2009, 2011, 2013, 2015, 2016

MIX
Paper from responsible sources
FSC™ C018179

Selected Street Index